SECRETS
OF SELF-
MASTERY

The Miracle of a Definite Chief Aim

The Power of the Master Mind

Secrets of Self-Mastery

The Napoleon Hill Success Course series™

SECRETS OF SELF-MASTERY

MITCH HOROWITZ

Inspired by the Teachings of
NAPOLEON HILL

An Approved Publication of the Napoleon Hill Foundation

MEDIA

Published by Gildan Media LLC
aka G&D Media
www.GandDmedia.com

Front cover design by Tom McKeveny

Interior design by Meghan Day Healey of Story Horse, LLC.

Library of Congress Cataloging-in-Publication Data
is available upon request

ISBN: 978-1-7225-0604-9

10 9 8 7 6 5 4 3 2 1

To my friends on the path

Contents

1

When Things Start Happening

We often hear that a single idea can change a life, or change the world. That's an inspiring thought—but it's incomplete.

Excellent application and execution of an idea are vital—perhaps even more so than the idea itself. A billionaire investor once told me: "There are a lot of great ideas out there. But when I invest I look for great execution more than great ideas. Great execution is much rarer than great ideas."

A friend whose startup this investor funded, which is now a worldwide consulting firm valued by the *Financial Times* at more than $700 million, said that this same financier told him: "I invest in people." That is not a bromide; it is a cast-iron principle. The investor wants to ensure that he's backing people who are consistently resourceful, decisive, capable of pivoting in almost any situation, and who are constitutionally averse to rigidity, sloppiness, guesswork, and apathy.

My wish is that *Secrets of Self-Mastery*, the third book in the Napoleon Hill Success Course series, will give you the tools to become the kind of person *worth* backing, financially and otherwise. Inspired by Hill's lessons, this book introduces, explores, and reinforces the widest range of self-development ideas found in his work, as well as more recent ideas that complement, reinforce, and expand on Hill's own. Each chapter includes Action Steps, which provide specific exercises and personal experiments.

I'd like you to regard *Secrets of Self-Mastery* as a field guide to personal effectiveness. Effectiveness, in short, means the ability to act on and progress toward a well-defined aim. Do you possess a definite aim in life? If you do—and if you hold to it with sincerity and passion—you have already accomplished a great deal. Most people lack a real aim, a point Hill emphasized and to which I return often in this book. Once you have determined your aim—which this book will also help you discover and clarify—you must possess the *personal effectiveness* to act on it. Without that, even the most finely honed idea will take you nowhere. Genius appears in action.

Some readers are surprised when they encounter Hill's *Think and Grow Rich* for the first time. They expect a strictly "mind power" approach to success. But for Hill, mental strategies, vital as they are, make up just one component of the long road toward success. Absolutely critical are organized planning and intelligent effort. People who never read *Think and Grow Rich*, or who just skim it, never learn this fact, and come away with a misimpression of Hill's program.

Writing in *Think and Grow Rich* in 1937, Hill put it this way with his emphasis in the original:

> KNOWLEDGE will not attract money, unless it is organized, and intelligently directed, through practical PLANS OF ACTION, to the DEFINITE END of accumulation of money. Lack of understanding of this fact has been the source of confusion to millions of people who falsely believe that "knowledge is power." It is nothing of the sort! Knowledge is only *potential* power. It becomes power only when, and if, it is organized into definite plans of action, and directed to a definite end.

For clarity, I should note that Hill's program can be used not only for money or entrepreneurship but for *any ethical aim*—which is to say one that respects the rights and needs of others, whatever your private goal. Hill described his program as comprising "not only the steps essential for the accumulation of money, but necessary for the attainment of *any definite goal*." He required only that your goal be clearly defined and uncompromisingly passionate.

I believe in bold promises—and I believe in supporting them. Hence, I never make a promise lightly to a reader, and I vow this to you: If you follow, practice, and persist in the methods in this book you will become the person who attracts resources, customers, backing, audience members, and opportunities.

I write this with confidence because I have experienced the effects of Hill's work myself. Although we all face our own complexities, as well as personal and sometimes social challenges, human nature is remarkably consistent. What transpires in the course of one person's experience can be applied in the life of another. In that spirit, let me describe how Hill's ideas have personally affected me.

For several years, I read *Think and Grow Rich* in a lackadaisical manner. As a longtime writer and publisher of self-help and metaphysical literature, I thought I already "got it"—that is, I believed that I had a handle on many of the motivational ideas and techniques in Hill's work. I was wrong. And it took a special turning point to make that clear to me.

In fall of 2013, I found myself facing a difficult crossroads in life and work. Personal challenges and industry shifts had shaken up my longstanding career as a publishing executive. A job that had once seemed familiar, secure, and even comfortable suddenly appeared threatened. I began to think seriously about how to broaden my work, not only as a publisher but also as a writer, speaker, and narrator—areas that I had hoped to grow further in, and upon which I knew I might someday depend for my sense of purpose and livelihood. As it happened, my instinct eventually proved right. Within about four years our company had a new corporate owner, shakeups ensued, and I was soon off on my own—and happily so thanks to *one key decision.*

In late 2013, I decided that it was time to return to *Think and Grow Rich*, but in a new way. I determined to approach the book with a sense of hardcore seriousness: no more skimming, cherry picking, or casual in-and-out reads. Rather, I approached the book and its ideas as though my life depended on it. I did every exercise from start to finish, even the ones I thought I already "got."

In Zen Buddhism this is called beginner's mind—and it is an immensely powerful approach to life or a specific project. I find an example in the career of the Austrian gun manufacturer Gaston Glock. Whatever your attitude toward guns, Glock created an enormously innovative handgun with no previous experience in either firearms design or manufacturing. The engineer had previously worked on curtain rods and field knives. In 1982, Glock succeeded in modeling his lightweight, plastic handgun—and surging past far more experienced competitors—because he approached its design unburdened by concepts of what "couldn't" be done, or what hadn't worked in the past. In effect, Glock used beginner's mind. This resulted in a dramatic innovation that shook up the munitions industry.*

Addressing the reader of *Think and Grow Rich*, Hill affirmed this beginner's mind approach: "Carry out these instructions as though you were a small child," that is, with eagerness, zeal, exuberance—and without prejudice. I took up this challenge. With pen in hand to highlight, underline, and take notes, I read Hill's book with a total sense of discovery. I prejudged nothing.

---

* You can read the definitive account in my friend Paul Barrett's 2012 book, *Glock*.

Slacked off on nothing. And followed each direction dutifully.

Things started happening. The speed and quality of my output not only improved in my writing, speaking, and narrating, but *I felt more like myself.* I was vastly more relaxed in public and private. I dressed and looked in ways that felt more comfortable and natural. My sense of purpose grew. My expertise broadened. In short, I had found my Definite Chief Aim, which for me was documenting metaphysical experience in history and practice.

Moreover, the work I was doing, probably as a combination of these factors, started paying better. My workmates, collaborators, and event venues improved in quality and resources. I am no financial wizard—but today I am a millionaire. I am one of the few writers I know of who makes his living solely from his craft. (And this at a time when income for full-time writers has dropped 42 percent since 2009, according to the Authors Guild.) I dress in T-shirts, jeans, leather boots and jackets, and I am covered with tattoos—in short, I live largely how I want. It didn't happen overnight and it didn't happen by accident. *Think and Grow Rich* was at the heart of it.

I believe that knowing what you want and taking a programmatic approach toward its fulfillment—mentally, spiritually, and in personal industriousness—will net results. The positive changes may not always arrive in the way you pictured. The channels of delivery may differ from your mind's eye. But things *will* occur. And when they do, you will need to possess a personal code and set of practices to sustain and build upon your progress. That is what this book is dedicated to.

Some readers may find the lessons in this book skewed too heavily in the direction of outer life, or conventional definitions of success. I am not insensitive to those concerns. But at this point in my search I believe that the highest expression of one's existence is through personal generativity and creativity, in whatever form is meaningful to the individual. I attach little value to terms like "inner" and "outer," or their equivalents, as I believe that all of life is one whole, and that whole is most evident in the individual's self-expressiveness. My wish is that this book will help you progress toward your highest sense of personal expression and generativity.

Action Step
Serve and Grow Rich

I say a lot in this book about aspiration and attainment. I also talk about the importance of pursuing your aim on an ethical basis. One of the best guides I know to *principled success* is a short, powerful book that is now nearly 150 years old.

Minister and educator Russell H. Conwell began delivering his famous motivational lecture and later book *Acres of Diamonds* in the 1870s. He recited it around the nation more than 6,152 times before his death in 1925. Conwell maintained his grueling speaking schedule in order to dedicate his lecture fees to opening a college for working-class students. That school today is Temple University in Philadelphia.

The motivational pioneer said he received inspiration for his landmark speech while traveling through the Middle East in 1869. An old Arab guide told him a story about a wealthy farmer who had squandered his fortune searching the world for diamonds—and dying a pauper before diamonds were finally discovered, on the very farm that he had abandoned to begin his quest.

Conwell insisted that success can be found where you stand—provided you possess the simplicity and soundness of character to see it. He taught that wealth comes from identifying and filling a genuine human need, and using your products and earnings to support the betterment of others, by which he meant doing business with transparency, truth-telling, and fair dealing. He did not mean this in some abstract or squishy way. Conwell believed that a seller should profit from customers and workers on a commensurate scale with how much they profited from him. Indeed, he believed that the seller of a truly sound product bestowed greater long-term benefit on the end user than he received. Conwell was writing in an age before our "disposable" economy, but I believe the principle remains applicable. The key is usefulness, quality, and reward.

You may be able to identify successful people who ignore these principles. They are easy enough to find. But, knowing a few personally, I maintain that they are privately miserable. I have witnessed the lives of retirees who built their success by walking across the skulls of others. I cannot determine that what I've witnessed is universal, but I have never personally seen happy endings in that story. There's no such thing as "just business." Life is a whole. You're either ethical or you're not.

Our path in this book is one of integrity, excellence, and reciprocity. If that sounds mawkish to you, pick up a different guidebook. You're in the wrong place.

We must relearn Russell H. Conwell's lessons: If you sincerely care enough about people to understand and provide for their needs, you will receive material rewards, which can be used to uplift yourself and those around you. This is the circuit of good business, sound ethics, and meaningful existence.

2

Mind Power and "the Zone"

The starting point of Napoleon Hill's program, and the turnkey to any definition of personal success, is the possession of a Definite Chief Aim. Hill considered the term so important that he capitalized it, a practice I continue. I often say that if you take only one message from Hill and the larger body of work that developed around his ideas, make it the cultivation of an impassioned, concrete, and actionable aim toward which you orient your existence. *Nothing* will do more to heighten your abilities and ensure your progress.

In selecting an aim, you must be starkly self-honest. The driving force behind the pursuit of an aim is passion. It cannot be faked. Without emotion at your back, you will not be able to sustain the energy and fortitude needed for success. You will get bored, you will drift— and you will fail. Hence, in selecting your aim there must be no self-deception, which quickly catches up with you.

I sometimes use this exercise: imagine that a genie offers to grant you your fondest wish—but on one condition: you must be completely sincere about what you want, or you will lose everything. It seems like a fearsome gambit; but, in some regards, this is the same bargain that life offers us. We receive something very close to what we most desire—*if* we want it badly enough and *if* it occupies the emotional center of our being. But if we deceive ourselves about what we really want, or fail to act on it, we either spin in circles or decline into listlessness. You may want to argue with this. I challenge you to scan your own life and that of your intimates; contrast your and their ideals with present circumstances. If you plumb the true depths of your wishes across long stretches of years you will begin to see a congruency between desire and circumstance. At least those circumstances over which we have control. And it can be unsettling. This is why self-honesty is so vital.

This lesson was unexpectedly reinforced for me through a remarkable work of cinema: a 1979 Soviet science-fiction film called *Stalker*. The Russian movie reached me in an unusual way. I was participating in a documentary series called *Cursed Films*, about horror movies that had been plagued by mishap, and around which a lore had developed. The series director asked me to watch and comment on *Stalker* (which, ironically, or perhaps true to form, never made it into the final cut). Both during production and after, *Stalker* was beset by serious tragedies, deaths, and accidents on and off set. I expected to discover a compellingly strange piece of cinematic history. But I found something more. *Stalker*, directed by Andrei Tarkovsky, is one of the most powerful and haunting movies I've ever seen. It offers a psychological message that ought to resound with anyone who works to apply creative-mind principles. The film also speaks with eerie accuracy to the points I've been making about desire, circumstance, and self-honesty.

The events in *Stalker* occur in what appears to be a post-apocalyptic landscape in central Russia, where the government has sealed off a forbidden area called the Zone. The Zone seems to be the site of a UFO landing or crash. Within the Zone exists a place called the Room; anyone who enters the Room is granted his or her deepest wishes. But venturing into the Zone is extremely dangerous. The military has cordoned off the area, and even those who make it inside often die within its environs, where the terrain is constantly morphing and deadly. For a fee, illegal guides called stalkers sneak in those who are intrepid or desperate enough to try. The previous stalker committed suicide and his protégé is the film's protagonist.

I'm about to reveal part of the ending, so you can watch the movie first and come back to this point—or venture with me into the Zone.

At the end we learn a secret: the Zone *does* grant your wishes—but it doesn't necessarily grant what you ask for, but rather what you *really want*. The Zone reads your subconscious. We discover that the previous stalker hanged himself in anguish after he ventured into the Zone with the intention of reviving his dead brother. But instead the stalker received heaps of money. Why?

Because he had deceived himself. *Despite what he told himself* he did not really wish for the return of his lost sibling so much as for riches. ("My consciousness wants the triumph of vegetarianism," one character quips. "My subconscious longs for a juicy steak.") The agony of confronting his true nature proved too much for the first stalker and he took his life.

One of the lessons I find in *Stalker* (and there are several) is that before you can embark on a meaningful journey of self-attainment you must first truly and starkly acknowledge what you really want. Without an intimate sense of self-understanding you confront yourself as a stranger. You may still receive what you want, but in ways that are alienating and disturbing. That can lead to personal disaster, as it did for the original stalker.

You can view the Zone as your own psyche; and yourself as the stalker seeking to probe and live out its truths. If you take seriously the creative potentials of thought, which the film does (and it's remarkable that it got past materialist, Soviet-era censors), you must take equally seriously the imperative of understanding who you really are—and what you want.

Do not be afraid of what you wish for. Never violate another or misrepresent yourself—but be radically honest. On this theme, I was unexpectedly touched by another movie, 2014's *Birdman* starring Michael Keaton. Seen from a certain perspective, the hero, played by Keaton, is an over-the-hill action star seeking renewed fame and artistic redemption by directing and starring in a Broadway drama.

"You're doing this," his daughter tells him, "because you're scared to death, like the rest of us, that you don't matter. And you know what? You're right."

Keaton's character, Riggan, is judged an egotist, out of touch with others around him, and somewhat hopelessly attempting to revive his career. In the end, however, the film flips that conventional premise on its head. Riggan comes to seem like a fairly decent, if conflicted, figure who is in his natural element in the spotlight. It is right and worthy for him to be on stage or screen—whereas those who criticize him gradually appear less compelling.

Although the movie explores the blurred lines between fantasy and reality, it also asks you to take a sustained look at your values—and to be certain that your ideals are authentic to you and not just handed-down truisms. Although the film suggests that artifice and reality have grown impossible to untangle, the hero Riggan is at least attempting some manner of self-establishment. Those who target him seem more and more like a dissatisfied mob.

Similar to Keaton's antagonists in the movie, critics of *Think and Grow Rich* and other success literature argue that positive-mind principles, motivational philosophy, and aspirational spirituality promote self-ishness and self-centeredness. I question that from years of experience.

During my time in spiritual publishing and writing, I've rarely seen anyone fixated on trying to manifest a temporal possession or some fleeting goodies. Rather, I encounter people coping with addictions, marital problems, career issues, illnesses, trouble paying the rent—things that are as real as life gets. But if someone *did* seek to manifest a shiny new car—just as Riggan seeks renewed fame—I would defend that person.

Who am I to judge what is natural, productive, and valuable in another's life? I can easily imagine someone growing up in squalor, and simply wanting to experience beautiful objects and surroundings or a well-made automobile. That may not be all that person wants, but it may represent something personally meaningful.

Like each of us, Keaton's character in *Birdman* possesses an instinctive if fitful sense of what he needs to reach his self-potential. He is tormented by the past, frustrated by the present, and trying to find his natural place as an actor. Neither he, nor anyone, should be made to feel shallow or "unspiritual" when longing to experience some sense of self-definition. Wishes are psychologically complex and intimate. We're sometimes cautioned that a wish conceals a deeper wound. There may be cases where that is true but with the passage of time I have come to realize that wishes are also a response to what the individual most deeply yearns to express. The sense of frustrated power that arises from a deterred wish can be agony. Hence, always aim for what truly matters to you. And never be too spiritually certain that the only things that matter are those we cannot see.

Life respects no halfway measures. The only aim that gets reached—whether the answer to a personal crisis, the achievement of a desire, or the search for some kind of inner understanding—is what you want with everything in you, without contradiction or division.

The hesitators, the undecided, those who commit to no path—they often just meander. I believe this is the meaning of the line from Revelation 3:16, which condemns the lukewarm: "So then because thou art lukewarm, and neither cold nor hot, I will spit thee out of my mouth."

In that sense, too, Napoleon Hill's approach places a demand on you, one that you may think you've risen to but have never really tried: to come to terms with precisely what you want. When you organize your thoughts in a certain way—with a fearless maturity and honesty— you may be surprised to discover your true desires. A person who considers himself spiritual may discover a wish for worldly attainment; someone who has labored to support the work of others may find that she has her own unfulfilled yearnings for self-expression, and that she wants to be in the spotlight; a person who is public-facing or outgoing may realize that he really desires solitude.

It is insufficient to tell yourself, as I once did, that you already know what you want. The things we repeat internally can take on a rote quality, obfuscating rather than revealing our desires. Taking a sustained and uninhibited inventory of what you wish for above all else—what appears literally in your dreams and at your unguarded moments—and then distilling it into a concise, specific written statement of purpose, will almost always net a surprising, if sometimes discomforting, discovery.

Attainment requires clarity. Yet our clarity gets muddied not only because of evasiveness but also because we elevate the means to the goal above the goal itself, and thus get distracted or diverted. Never confuse means with ends. Sometimes we mistakenly perceive just *one kind* of job or *one form* of recognition as the channel through which our good must arrive. When we get fixated on an exclusive method of delivery we may block out or fail to recognize other possibilities. (I deal more fully with this in chapter eleven, "The 10-Day Miracle Challenge.").

Be specific about what you want—but don't get boxed in by the perceived means of how it must arrive. In that vein, I end this chapter with a lesson in clarity and flexibility that I received from Dean Radin, a psychical researcher at the Institute of Noetic Sciences in Northern California. Everything changed for Dean when he got clear about what he needed to complete an important experiment. Here, with my condensation, is Dean's story:

> In 2009, we upgraded the EEG equipment in our lab to prepare for an experiment. We ran the experiment and collected a ton of data. Then the analysis phase began. I surveyed software suitable for analyzing EEG data and found one that looked particularly good called EEGLAB. It uses Matlab, a high-end programming language.
>
> My initial idea was to find a college student familiar with Matlab and willing to learn how to use EEGLAB. I asked my research assistant, Leena, to see if she could find someone like that. She asked me to be clearer on exactly what I was looking for.

What I really wanted was an experienced neuroscientist familiar with EEGLAB, willing to analyze the data from our experiment for free, and also willing to collaborate on the kind of psi study that falls far outside the parameters that most neuroscientists are willing to entertain. I wasn't sure such a person existed.

Leena said not to worry about it.

Two days later I received an email from someone who had attended a talk I gave a few years before. He wanted to visit our lab. Turns out, this fellow was not only a bona fide academic neuroscientist (from UC San Diego), and not only an expert with Matlab, and not only wanted to volunteer his assistance—he was also the person *who developed and maintained EEGLAB!*

This is just one example of a dozen or so striking synchronicities I've experienced, all of which related to my gaining crystal clarity on exactly what I wanted. After gaining clarity, it generally takes a few days to a few weeks for the vision to manifest.

It is important to note that Dean's actualization was preceded by a tremendous amount of prior work and sweat equity. Never neglect that point, which we will explore further.

Action Step
The Three-Step Miracle

Many of us go through life fuzzily thinking that we know what we want: a new house, a loving mate, a better job, and so on. But the things that we repeat inside can take on a habitual tone, obfuscating rather than revealing our true yearnings.

Have you ever sat down, in a mature manner, stripped of all convention, and asked yourself what you *really* want?

A perfect method for doing this appears inside a special little book that I have given away hundreds of copies of. It is a 28-page pamphlet, published anonymously in 1926 under the title *It Works*. The author was a Chicago sales executive who wrote under the alias R.H.J., for Roy Herbert Jarrett.

It Works distills a program of creative-mind metaphysics into three very simple steps. These steps work only if approached with your whole being. They are:

1. Carefully devise a handwritten list of what you really want from life. Take your time with it. It could take days or weeks. Be entirely uninhibited.

2. Once you feel that your list is well honed, commit it to a notepad or index card. Carry it with you. Read it just as you wake up; again at midday; and

once more before you go to sleep. You can read it other times, as well. Think about it always.

3. Tell no one what you are doing. This is so you remain steady in your resolve. Silence is your ally. Bob Dylan put it this way in an interview on *60 Minutes* in 1994: "It's a feeling you have that you know something about yourself nobody else does. The picture you have in your mind of what you're about, will come true; it's kind of a thing you're gonna have to keep to your own self. Because it's a fragile feeling and you put it out there and somebody will kill it, so it's best to keep that all inside."

Then, in whatever way you like, express gratitude as results arrive.

How can something so simple really work? Because this exercise pushes us to do something that we think we do all the time but rarely try: *honestly come to terms with our truest desires.* A single act of passionate self-clarification can reprogram your interior mind to function like a kind of homing device; you will begin to refine relationships, activities, and thoughts to fit the needs of your desires.

If you don't know about *It Works*, this Action Step may mark a turning point in your search. And if you do know it, I hope that what I write here will return you to it.

3

What Artists Know

Napoleon Hill had a keen understanding of the role of desire in the life of an artist—and how crucial desire is in any form of artistic or creative success. In his chapter on "Desire" in *Think and Grow Rich*, he noted the story of Ernestine Schumann-Heink (1861–1936), a celebrated opera performer:

> As this chapter was being completed, news came of the death of Mme. Schumann-Heink. One short paragraph in the news dispatch gives the clue to this unusual woman's stupendous success as a singer. I quote the paragraph, because the clue it contains is none other than DESIRE.
>
> Early in her career, Mme. Schumann-Heink visited the director of the Vienna Court Opera, to have him test her voice. But, he did not test

it. After taking one look at the awkward and poorly dressed girl, he exclaimed, none too gently, "With such a face, and with no personality at all, how can you ever expect to succeed in opera? My good child, give up the idea. Buy a sewing machine, and go to work. YOU CAN NEVER BE A SINGER."

Never is a long time! The director of the Vienna Court Opera knew much about the technique of singing. He knew little about the power of desire, when it assumes the proportion of an obsession. If he had known more of that power, he would not have made the mistake of condemning genius without giving it an opportunity.

This brings me to a revelation about performer Michael Jackson. I write this observation with some trepidation. I realize that the pop legend is controversial today. But I also believe that every artist, of whatever type, deserves to be remembered for his or her best work.

In that sense, I am sharing an extraordinary handwritten note of Michael's. It is pure inspirational mind metaphysics, or what is often called New Thought. Michael's note comports well with the outlook of Napoleon Hill. What's more, his note beckons you, the reader, to complete it—he actually left a blank space at the end to enter your own aim. To my knowledge, this short piece of writing has never before appeared in book form.

Michael was no stranger to mind metaphysics or the power of suggestion. The philosophy made up a significant part of his artistic outlook. In earlier research, I learned that Michael's favorite book was James Allen's

1903 mind-power classic, *As a Man Thinketh*. Michael told a childhood friend in Philadelphia that Allen's meditation was his "favorite book in the world."** Many of the twentieth century's leading American writers of motivational thought—from Napoleon Hill to Norman Vincent Peale—read and noted the influence of *As a Man Thinketh*. Dale Carnegie said the book had "a lasting and profound effect on my life."

I discovered Michael's note in its original form on a 2019 visit to Atlantic City, New Jersey, where it was on display at the Hard Rock Hotel & Casino. It is a handwriting-authenticated but undated document that Michael penned in cursive on the back of a laundry-service order form.

Michael's note suggests what may have drawn him to *As a Man Thinketh*, and the passage comports with other things the pop star wrote about creativity. Below I have transcribed his message exactly as it appeared in his original handwriting.

Remember: this message is unfinished. Michael left space at the end for the reader to complete it. This is your opportunity to share in an icon's thought process. I hope you will use this passage not only as insight into one person's journey, but also as a tool in your own:

> I have learned that it is what you put in your mind Mentally what you think and do, that makes your person. And you can put any Mental object in this mind and it will bring it

---

* His comment is from "Radnor Family Had Inside Look at Michael Jackson" by Patti Mengers, *Delaware County Daily Times* (PA), June 28, 2009.

into reality. So this means, we can program ourselves to be the people we want to be, whatever the subject matter is, live in it by a Mental physical program, a system of learning and doing, studying all the greats in that field and becoming greater. My program will consist of, _____.

I also want to note the statement of another pop icon from a different generation, Sammy Davis Jr. Davis's memoir *Yes I Can*, which appeared in my birth year of 1965, is, on its surface, the autobiography of a great stage performer. But the book is also, without intending to be, a strikingly powerful exploration of mind-causation and human potential. *Yes I Can* demonstrates how a biography can transcend its genre and become more than the story of a life, but the story of all lives with universal lessons.

It is insufficient to call *Yes I Can* inspiring; it is a biographical lesson in the philosophy of self-development. Davis describes hardships and brutalities that most of us will never know: beatings at the hands of racists, slurs hurled at him even at the height of his success, pains of hunger while dancing as a child on the segregated vaudeville circuit.

While recounting his life and breakthrough, Davis, like Michael, provided insight into his mental methodology. When a girl stood up a teen Sammy on a date, he wrote: "I closed my eyes … I was headlining at the Paramount. She was sitting up front waving at me. . . ." He later headlined around the world.

When his family was too poor to stock the fridge, his father pasted pictures of food inside. He reminded them of what life would be.

At a turning point in Davis's life, a rabbi told him: "Man is made in God's image and therefore is endowed with unlimited potential ... his most important responsibility is to live up to whatever is within him." Davis later said: "This has been my thinking all my life"—and he converted to Judaism.

Following a car accident in which he lost an eye, Davis prayed: "Dear God, I don't know why you gave me another chance. I don't know why you want me here or why you gave me this talent. And I know I haven't used it the way you must have intended for me to use it. But I want to ... Please show me what to do." He soon became one of the greatest stage entertainers of his era.

The north star of Davis's life appeared to him when he left the military after World War II. At that time, he made an inner vow that shaped his destiny:

> I'd learned a lot in the army and I knew that above all things in the world I had to become so big, so strong, so important, that those people and their hatred could never touch me. My talent was the only thing that made me a little different from everybody else, and it was all that I could hope would shield me because I was different.
>
> I'd weighed it all, over and over again: What have I got? No looks, no money, no education. Just talent. Where do I want to go? I want to be treated well. I want people to like me, and to be

decent to me. How do I get there? There's only one way I can do it with what I have to work with. I've got to be a star! I have to be a star like another man has to breathe.

Decades later, KISS front man Paul Stanley made a strikingly similar statement about how he emerged from a childhood marked by partial-deafness and the birth defect of missing a right ear. The rock performer spoke in terms similar to Davis's, telling an interviewer in 2019: "I was a little, unpopular chubby kid with a deformed ear and not very socially skilled, and I wanted to create this persona that would make me sought after, and make the people who I didn't think were nice to me envious—'oh, we shoulda been nice to him'..." I admired Stanley's honesty.

If you have a wish for fame, what drives it? Whatever it is, do not be ashamed of it or embarrassed out of it. The very possession of the wish is validity enough. Pursue it—and see. We often hear that fame and riches will not make you happy. But those sentiments frequently come from people who have neither. Or sometimes we hear them from people who *have* attained life's pinnacle, and found it lacking. In any case, neither observation dictates what's intimately right for *you*. Find out.

Action Step
The Power of Maybe

All of the performers mentioned in this chapter functioned from a place of self-belief. The assumption that you *can* do something must be wed to skills that you either possess or can attain; but healthful self-belief is vital in either case.

In this vein, I sometimes attempt a personal experiment, which I invite you to try. I approach a favorite book of mind metaphysics and attempt to free myself of all preconceptions surrounding its ideas. How would these ideas affect me, I ask, if I were encountering them for the first time? If they were true? How would it expand my sense of possibility?

Remarkable things can emerge from a feeling of fresh possibility. Philosopher William James (1842–1910) called it the sense of *maybe*. He wrote this in 1895:

> The "scientific" life itself has much to do with maybes, and human life at large has everything to do with them. So far as man stands for anything, and is productive or originative at all, his entire vital function may be said to deal with maybes. Not a victory is gained, not a deed of faithfulness or courage is done, except upon a maybe … It is only by risking our persons from one hour to another that we live at all. And often enough our faith beforehand in an uncer-

tified result *is the only thing that makes the result come true.* Suppose, for instance, that you are climbing a mountain and have worked yourself into a position from which the only escape is by a terrible leap. Have faith that you can successfully make it, and your feet are nerved to its accomplishment. But mistrust yourself, and think of all the sweet things you have heard the scientists say of *maybes*, and you will hesitate so that, at last, all unstrung and trembling, and launching yourself in a moment of despair, you roll in the abyss. In such a case ... the part of wisdom as well as of courage is to *believe what is in the line of your needs*, for only by the belief is the need fulfilled.

James saw belief in a result or possibility as the core factor in determining how or whether you experience a given outcome. Hence, belief in the power of your mental images can, in itself, increase their efficacy. Try this experiment. The outcome may surprise you.

4

Leave the Ruins

"Resolve to throw off the influences of any unfortunate environment," Napoleon Hill wrote, "and to build your own life to ORDER." For many years—indeed for most of my life—I've had difficulty living by this principle. I developed a lifelong habit, probably stemming from my earliest years, of trying to wrestle resources, positive support, or other desired things from people or situations that could not provide them. Yet, despite the evidence, I couldn't let go. To feel a sense of self-possession, however, we must sometimes let go—and do so decisively.

"Part of being powerful is being able to walk away," as a close friend puts it. This doesn't mean behaving impulsively, rashly, or rejecting compromise. (So long as a compromise doesn't sully the core of what you're trying to create, it is a necessary part of every relationship, professional or otherwise.) But knowing what you want in life, and what you *won't* compromise on—such as a supportive work environment or an honest boss—means knowing when to say no. This may be directed at a person, a relationship, a business opportunity, or a job. What you say no to is as self-defining as what you agree to.

A friend once told me that she had been invited to join the cast of a questionable reality TV show. The show assembled various spiritual practitioners to live in a house together to see how they would get along. (You can only imagine the outcome.) She was uneasy and didn't know how to respond. I told her that a no and a yes are equally powerful provided they come from a place of integrity. She turned the producers down, and never looked back. She felt at peace with her decision not to join a near-certain exploitative show. She also felt good that she delivered her response expeditiously and confidently.

I faced a similar quandary shortly before this writing. A spiritual organization for which I had done writing and speaking, and to which I had contributed a book and its profits, told me that after a ten-year relationship they were expunging me. At issue was esoteric spiritual subject matter that I dealt with outside of my work for them, and which some members found off-putting. I was saddened and surprised. But, again, the break arrived as a sign that I could not linger where I once had been comfortable. Growth, expansion, and intellectual freedom were needed. I recalled the words of Ralph Waldo Emerson toward the end of his 1841 essay *Compensation*, where the philosopher noted the tough necessity of breaking with the past:

We cannot part with our friends. We cannot let our angels go. We do not see that they only go out, that archangels may come in. We are idolaters of the old. We do not believe in the riches of the soul, in its proper eternity and omnipresence. We do not believe there is any force in today to rival or recreate that beautiful yesterday. We linger in the ruins of the old tent, where once we had bread and shelter and organs, nor believe that the spirit can feed, cover, and nerve us again. We cannot again find aught so dear, so sweet, so graceful. But we sit and weep in vain. The voice of the Almighty saith, 'Up and onward for evermore!' We cannot stay amid the ruins. Neither will we rely on the new; and so we walk ever with reverted eyes, like those monsters who look backwards.

The pains and doubts to which Emerson refers expose a need for growth and movement. Movement itself is compensatory. It is a natural and metaphysical law that events conspire to force organic life beyond its boundaries if it must outgrow them to thrive. This is why the roots of a tree can burst through layers of concrete. Waters overrun their banks. You, too, are forced past limitations—a relationship, a workplace, a friendship—in ways that can at first seem painful and jarring; but, looking back, you will often discover that these breaks represented pathways of growth.

Always compromise for purposes of quality or to honor positive relationships—but never to maintain ties that violate your deepest standards. You must try to chart your life according to certain non-negotiable principles. And you must also live with the consequences—so be careful. I always tell people: "Don't be a hero after you cash the check." If someone pays you to do something, you have an obligation to accommodate him. If you cannot live with that obligation, then it is your job to return the money or otherwise make it right. But I can assure you: it is better to risk exiting a bad road than to wonder at the healthier turn never taken. Hence, I invite you to join me in the oath below, which I ask you to sign and date.

"I Swear"

I SWEAR to lead my own life, as strongly as possible.

I SWEAR to be responsible for my own finances, health, and wellbeing.

I SWEAR to dedicate myself to my children or those in my care, as well as to my household obligations, without anyone's prompting, list-making, or date-keeping.

I SWEAR to first search on my own for answers and solutions, in matters large and small, before burdening others.

I SWEAR not to seek comfort, approval, or safety in the perceptions and responses of others, real or imagined.

I SWEAR to respect myself socially,
professionally, and intimately, and to honor
my expectations, wishes, and boundaries
in relationships.

I SWEAR that while striving toward my best,
most forward-looking life, I will also endeavor
to honor and respect others, to see their point
of view, and to treat people fairly.

I SWEAR to offer authentic solidarity and loyalty
to friends, collaborators, and workmates, but
never to accept other people's manipulations
or unwarranted demands.

I SWEAR to be responsible for my own
existence to the fullest extent possible.

I now sign and date this pledge and vow to live
by it every hour—and when I fail, to return to it,
again and again, for the rest of my life.

_____   _____

[signature]   [date]

Action Step
Therapy and the Written Word

Israeli physicist and mind-body therapist Moshe Feldenkrais (1904–1984) observed that you should always be able to write down at least three solutions to any problem, whether situational or psychological. When faced with adversity, stop and enumerate your options in an unemotional manner. Write them down. There are almost always dimensions of possibility that you have not considered, and depths of insight you have not used.

To prime this process, I want to share the following letter I received from a reader:

Mitch, on a personal note, my oldest son who is 19 struggles with the double-sided coin of depression and anxiety. Which author, book, or audio, do you recommend him to read first? Maybe there are three books to read in a certain order? If you could jump-start me with at least the first one that would be helpful. I really do believe New Thought can be lifesaving and life-changing for him.

I agreed, and ruminated on my correspondent's request. First and foremost, I do not believe in a one-size-fits all approach to depression, anxiety, or other crises. I endorse a "D-Day approach" to personal problems—throw everything into the struggle: meditation, prayer, exercise, therapy, and, where applicable, medication. Physical and emotional health are deeply intimate; let no one proscribe or dictate what works for you.

That said, I deeply believe that inspirational and motivational thought are part of the solution to emotional struggles. Here is how I replied:

Hi _____, I've been considering your question. I recommend these works: 1) Neville Goddard's *At Your Command*, 2) Ernest Holmes's *This Thing Called You*, and 3) Earl Nightingale's *The Strangest Secret*.

You could actually reverse my suggested reading order: Earl's message is the simplest. It comes down to his youthful realization: "You become what you think about." Earl discovered that that insight runs throughout all the world's religious and ethical philosophies. Ernest's message is the metaphysical version of the "good news," centering on the mind's creative powers. (An interesting thing about this list is that whatever your reading order, Ernest is at its center.) And, finally, Neville provides the most epic vision of what we can become. He teaches that your mind is literally God the Creator, and your thoughts and emotions are the foundation of every circumstance.

There is one further ingredient that ensures the efficacy of this or any metaphysical problem-solving program: absolute passion for self-change. Without that, nothing is possible; with it, every idea becomes a key to your liberation.

5

The Art of Being Seen

Napoleon Hill emphasized the importance of getting noticed for the right things you are doing. You cannot benefit from opportunities unless other people, including people of influence, know about you and your accomplishments. This does not mean becoming a slave to social media or a tiresome self-promoter. (Although I must grudgingly note that a not-insignificant number of self-promoters meet with success.) On a more noble level, you must honestly and plainly make clear to others your output and enthusiasms.

A friend who works in audio publishing once told me she was having difficulty getting noticed at work. At a certain point, she realized that she had been concealing her enthusiasm and dedication. This may have arisen from some bad career advice she received years earlier, and had acted on. As she told it:

Today, a coworker sat in on an audiobook recording session I was engineering. At the end she looked at me and said, "Wow, I've never seen you so passionate about a project before."

That may sound like a compliment; but I didn't hear it that way.

Yes, it's true that I was in love with the project. But my love for this particular project was small compared to the passion I have felt for so many other projects that I have engineered during my past decade in the audiobook industry.

In fact, the passion I felt for that one project was basically the same that I have felt for nearly every project on which this colleague and I have collaborated. So—*why did she think that this case was so exceptional?*

I now I realize that, while I have shared my enthusiasm for work with friends, I have rarely shared it with my coworkers. Is it any wonder that I have not been promoted or even received a significant raise after ten dedicated years? (Indeed, today my debt exceeds my yearly income.)

My coworker was right: I *am* passionate and deeply curious; but I am this way about nearly *every book*; I also care about the talent and producers. Her expression of surprise finally made me realize that people simply haven't seen this side of me.

As of now, this changes.

My coworkers must see what my friends already have: that I am exuberant over nearly everything I do.

I don't know *why* I haven't been sharing my passion at work. It may have been because years ago a manager told me that the way to get ahead in corporate publishing is to "keep your head down." At the time, I thought that was good, practical advice. It was not. It was a formula for mediocrity. And, most importantly, it is not *me*.

In the past, I have maintained a deep but quiet dedication in recording sessions. I think of every detail: I care about the needs of people working on the project; I show up early and prepared; I see things from all perspectives; I double-check facts and pronunciations; I do independent research; I am organized; I am innovative—and, yes, *I am very passionate*. But—I wrongly believed that these traits might seem obsessive or annoying.

No more. I am done hiding my passion. I want people to know. All people. If they like it, great; and if not, still great. *Because I am being me.*

My friend's realization was right. The act of "keeping your head down" is feckless and self-defeating. And it shows poor work ethics. People who keep their heads down never learn; they rarely take responsibility; and they often make others carry extra burdens for them. Have you ever worked with someone who asks the same kinds of routine questions over and over, no matter how long they've been on the job? As a friend once put it, "For those people every day is the first day." In actuality they are not asking real questions, which involve listening for meaningful responses and integrating them into your efforts. Rather they are passively dislocating responsibility; bogus or frivolous questions are a way of "task dumping" onto other people.

Taking responsibility and getting noticed are far more likely, in the long run, to place you in the stream of advancement. If you accept responsibility there may be times when you get saddled with blame. There may be occasions where blame is unfairly placed on you. But even this can remind you of a healthy practice: taking credit when it is given. One time I saw a publicist at a publishing meeting get complimented for scoring an important media hit. "I didn't really do anything..." he began to explain. An executive turned around to him and whispered: "*Take credit.* You'll get blame when you don't deserve it, too."

In short: be noticed. The spotlight is often where the action is.

Action Step
Social Media Pitfalls and Principles

Social media is, of course, an indelible part of life. To abstain from it is the equivalent a generation ago of not having a telephone. You cannot function in commerce and culture without social media.

I've asked myself many times: What is an appropriate way to behave on social media? I want to reach people, but I don't want to be a gutless self-promoter. I've also seen, as we all have, routine yet still-shocking instances where people erupt into anger or violent sarcasm. Such behavior taints reputations and damages our culture. (One way to reduce the heat: as a rule, avoid all-caps and ironic quotation marks.)

A stranger once told me over social media that she needed one of my books to get through a difficult period. The book hadn't gone on sale yet but I sent her a free copy, signed and postage paid. Several months later, wisely or not, I posted a mildly contentious comment about a certain office-holder; this same person disagreed—and she vented at me with unrestrained vitriol. It was a harsh window onto human nature.

I do not swear off contentious topics on social media. But I do try to avoid caustic cracks and personal attacks. I find that much of today's sarcasm is overused, scolding, and depleting. Of course, sarcasm has its place. It can be funny; it can be revealing. But it has gotten so overused on social media that it has transformed into something it was never intended to be: the language of everyday life. Sarcasm-as-default renders so many encounters needlessly angry.

I sometimes witness people saying things on social media that are so over the line that I fear our culture has lost its capacity for moral embarrassment. I'm concerned about that. If we don't start to take back some yardage, we're going to lose it all. This is one of the reasons I discourage anonymity online, because I think you should have to stand by what you say.

I once did a streaming video with the *Washington Post* about the eightieth anniversary of Dale

Carnegie's self-help classic, *How to Win Friends and Influence People.* I mentioned that our digital generation must relearn that book's lessons. We should never put ourselves above such lessons, or think that we're too sophisticated for a book like Carnegie's. In fact, we need the book even more today because of how frivolously disinhibited many people feel over social media, emails, and texts. People routinely fail to pair up consequences with words. That's a reality this generation is conscripted to relearn.

Let's face it: social media grants you limitless opportunities to behave caustically. When these opportunities arrive, resist them. Abstaining from a verbal pile-on, snarky comment, or minor insult is an act of rebellion against a digital culture that sells anger back to us. Social media giants profit from every spleen-fueled comment chain. In its aggregate, vitriol may be the biggest online commodity. Be among the minority who do not contribute to the anger economy. You'll mark yourself as independent and effective.

6

Meeting Your Hidden Self

"The turning point in the lives of those who succeed," Napoleon Hill wrote in *Think and Grow Rich*, "usually comes at the moment of some crisis, through which they are introduced to their 'other selves.'"

I take this statement very seriously and consider it true—perhaps literally so. If you're like me, you often walk around feeling like there are "two of you"—dual selves fighting for dominance. And I believe you are right: There are, in a sense, two personas struggling within us all, like Jacob and Esau.

We experience this when we feel ourselves divided between ordinary life and peak possibility. People often harbor the feeling that they *could* become a writer, or *could* get straight As, or *could* excel at work, or *could* find a positive relationship . . . if only they were able to freely throw themselves upon the energies of their higher, better, more formidable doppelgänger, waiting to be released. This possibility is real, but it is rarely or only fleetingly exercised.

Years ago on a bright winter day I climbed to the top of an abandoned watchtower along the banks of the Charles River near Waltham, Massachusetts. It was shortly before the full-on start of my writing career. Feeling possessed by something unnamable, I stood at the top of that tower and vowed with everything in me that I would succeed as a writer. My pledge was a totalizing experience: it felt physically, emotionally, and intellectually tangible. At that moment something *else* welled up within me; some other presence become palpable. Something occupied me. My success proceeded steadily from that time forward.

I had another such experience more recent to this writing. I was standing at the center of a lobby in a beautifully restored neo-futuristic hotel in New York City. The place was a marvel of visionary design and epic architecture. It represented something to me about how I wanted to live. Again, I felt suffused with an unnamed sense of inner possession, and I made a personal vow, summoning every aspect of my physicality and psyche, about how I wanted to live—about the beauty, people, and environment I wanted to exist among. Standing there in stillness, I felt like a different self.

Many modern fiction writers and psychologists, not to mention their ancient and folkloric forebearers, have posited the existence of this "other self." Psychologist Carl Jung famously called it the shadow, which he identified as a fount of unacknowledged desires and proclivities; if acknowledged and integrated into your day-to-day consciousness, these shadow traits can lead to the growth of untapped powers, confidence, and abilities. For fantasy writer Robert Louis Stevenson, the other self was the malevolent "Mr. Hyde," a feral counterpart to the refined and likeable persona of Dr. Jekyll. For Edgar Allan Poe, the other side was represented by "William Wilson," the title of Poe's 1839 short story in which his protagonist, the debauched Wilson, grows up alongside an uncanny double who shares his name, appearance, and birthdate, and who eventually turns out to be the maleficent hero's alienated conscience.

Many fiction writers, like Stephen King in his 1989 novel, *The Dark Half*, see the other self as a figure of repressed violence and evil. But that reflects only one sliver of the split-self riddle of human nature. More important for our purposes, your counter-self can be a figure of relative fearlessness, effectiveness, and ability. Napoleon Hill wrote this intriguing passage in *Think and Grow Rich* about short story writer O. Henry (1862–1910):

> O. Henry discovered the genius which slept within his brain, after he had met with great misfortune, and was confined to a prison cell in Columbus, Ohio. Being FORCED, through misfortune, to become acquainted with his "other self," and to use his IMAGINATION, he discovered himself to be a great author instead of a miserable criminal and outcast. Strange and varied are the ways of life, and stranger still are

the ways of Infinite Intelligence, through which men are sometimes forced to undergo all sorts of punishments before discovering their own brains, and their own capacity to create useful ideas through imagination.

One of the oddest inspirational works ever written, *The Magic Story*, featured this theme of a positive double, which author Frederick Van Rensselaer Dey (1861–1922) called your "plus-entity." In Dey's brief and strangely compelling instructional tale from 1900 he described the life of a down-and-out seventeenth-century crafts-man who discovers that a haunting presence, or other self, is hovering around his periphery. The hero finds that his counter-self is a real part of him, one that is "calm, steadfast, and self-reliant." As soon as he comes to identify, literally, with his plus-entity, his life is hap-pily transformed. "Make a daily and nightly companion of your plus-entity," the hero counsels.

As it happens, the author Dey's life was less than happy. After a middling and prolific career writing pulp crime fiction, including the popular Nick Carter detec-tive tales, the wearied writer shot himself to death in 1922. He left behind a stoic suicide note, asking only that his older brother be taken care of. Dey's widow, Haryot Holt Dey, was herself a notable writer and suffragist who lived until 1950. To use the terms of Dey's own allegory, the author succumbed to his "minus-entity."

How can you get in touch with your stronger plus-entity?

Dress the Part

Never neglect the power of simple things. The manner in which you dress and comport yourself has tremendous impact on your psyche. Most people instinctively sense this without fully acting on it. (This is one reason why the process of transitioning can feel enormously liberating to a transgender person.) Become a thespian, trying out, perhaps subtly at first, different styles of dress, makeup, accessories, and body art.

Feed Your Other Self

Allow yourself to become immersed in music, movies, and media that feed your sense of power and self-agency. As an example, consider the elegant but deadly robot named David in the 2012 science fiction movie *Prometheus*. Watch or re-watch the movie and take note of how David studiously models his persona after the cinematic Lawrence of Arabia. Although brief, these scenes are no passing trifle; they are mini-models of the kinds of self-making we all engage in, sometimes without awareness.

Talk Like It

Consider the manner in which you speak. I once knew a crime reporter at a newspaper in upstate New York who had a slight build and appearance—but he spoke in a commanding, self-confident bass voice. It earned him the respect of the police and his newsroom colleagues.

Whether natural or affected (I could never tell), his voice altered his entire persona.

Find a Manifesto

You may be deterred from reading *The Magic Story* given its author's tragic end. Do not be. Read it tonight. (You can buy a copy digitally or find it online.) Make its lessons your own. Dey possessed a keen instinct for human nature, including its shadowy and occultic paths to power. If that book doesn't speak to you, select another from the works I've mentioned, or find ones of your own.

Stand for Something

The chief cause of mediocrity is purposelessness. We are never more aroused, sensitive, and capable than when we are striving for something. What are you striving for? A watch-the-clock job and entertainment won't bring out more than your most average traits. Once again, you must find a Definite Chief Aim in life. You should never be embarrassed by your aim. Your aim can be outwardly focused or intimate. It requires no one's approval—it must be distinctly your own. The only tragedy is not having one.

Since earliest childhood, you have probably felt, as I have, that you are two selves. Select the one that builds you. It represents a more powerful choice than may at first appear.

Action Step
The Psychology of Clothing

Part of discovering your other self involves cultivating the right outer appearance—one that you are comfortable with and that speaks to who you really are, or wish to be. Shortly before this writing, I "took a meeting" (as Hollywood people say) at a media hotspot in New York City. I was worried that I'd be underdressed. But when I arrived, I discovered that all the men there were dressed more or less like fifteen-year-olds. I fit right in. In fact, I seemed mature by comparison. I wear T-shirts, jeans, and leather boots and jackets. I'm covered in tattoos. It's just what makes me comfortable.

That's why I want to emphasize the psychology of clothing.

Most self-help teaches that change begins within. But that does not mean that the inner world is the only, or even the primary, field on which we function. A subtle interplay exists between inner and outer. If you want to boost your self-confidence and attract positive attention, working on your outer appearance will make a significant difference.

Past generations were taught to "dress for success"—which generally meant suits and shined shoes for men, and professional dresses or pantsuits for women. But today's secret to dressing for success is adopting a daily "uniform" that makes you feel self-possessed or at home wherever you are.

Napoleon Hill emphasized this point in *The Law of Success*: "An appearance of prosperity attracts attention, with no exceptions whatsoever. Moreover, a look of prosperity attracts 'favorable attention,' because the one dominating desire in every human heart is to be prosperous." I would update Hill's advice by substituting the word "independence" for "prosperity." Today's dominating desire is to be self-directed, independent, and—yes—prosperous.

Remember what Steve Jobs chose as Apple's slogan? "Think Different." The digital pioneer wore a studied daily uniform of black turtlenecks, jeans, and New Balance sneakers. (According to biographer Walter Isaacson, Jobs owned hundreds of the same articles of clothing for his uniform.) His appearance said: I make my own rules; I think different.

In a classic episode of *The Simpsons*, a teacher tells young Lisa: "Being tough comes from inside. First step—change your outside." It's a joke, of course. But like all good jokes it conceals a truth: the outside reinforces who you are within.

As you adopt the clothing or look that makes you comfortable, or brings out traits you want to cultivate, you'll find that your tone and voice change; your creative expressiveness also changes and improves as an artist, writer, or presenter. An enticing testimony to this power appears in a memoir by KISS drummer Peter Criss and his cowriter Larry "Ratso" Sloman, *Makeup to Breakup: My Life in and Out of KISS*. Criss and Sloman recall the transformative effect that stage makeup had on band members when they were creating their look and sound in the early 1970s:

> What's scary is that the more we got into roles and the makeup, the more we actually became our alter egos. Once we ditched the female eye shadow and eyeliner and lipstick and actually created these four characters with full-on theatrical makeup, we transformed into different entities. Gene [Simmons] morphed right into a demon. That little Hasidic boy was nowhere to be found when the Demon took over Gene's brain. He would spit right into our roadies' faces. Just plodding around on those platform shoes, which added to his natural height, he exuded menace. People would literally cringe in fear when he came near... Gene once told me that if he could leave his makeup on all the time and never leave that persona, he would do it.

That may sound a bit gruesome but it greatly heightened Simmons' sense of character and theatricality. Other members of the band had similar, if interpersonally milder, experiences: each came to occupy his character and felt elevated confidence, stage presence, and a sense of personal identity. In varying ways, this can happen to you, whether on or off stage, when you are mindful of the intimate connection between outer appearance and the inner you.

As a friend of mine puts it: "Everything tells a story." What story do you want to tell about yourself?

7

Power with Purpose

You may have noticed a lot of books on attaining power making the rounds in recent years. I find some of these books distasteful, making *The Art of the Deal* sound like Marcus Aurelius. I discourage lessons in pursuing success without honor or ethics. I don't believe in taking credit for other people's efforts or ideas, intimidating acquaintances, withholding information, or being a general sneak.

Mine may be the minority opinion—but there *is* a better way. And it sits on history's forgotten bookshelf. I am referring to an obscure and easily underestimated work first published in 1963: *The Million Dollar Secret Hidden in Your Mind.* Its author was a jack-of-all-trades success guru, pitchman, and pop-occultist named Anthony Norvell (1908–1990). The bicoastal writer and speaker was briefly known in the late 1940s and '50s for renting out Carnegie Hall on Sundays, where he addressed audiences as "The Twentieth-Century Philosopher." (Wittgenstein, move over.)

For all his hyperbole and sometimes feverishly titled self-help potboilers like *Psychic Dreamology* and *The Mystical Power of Pyramid Astrology*, Norvell did make sound points about the non-exploitative pursuit of personal success. This may reveal as much about him as a slightly dodgy character with a good heart as it does about the below-the-belt standards of our own era.

A generation before today's spate of power-grabbing books, this Hollywood–New York mystic attempted to popularize many of the same general principles, but without plate-licking, cut-you-off-in-traffic trickiness—and with an emphasis on legitimate personal growth.

In particular, I recommend his chapter "How to Seek and Win the Aid of Important People." Writing with more edge and bluntness than Dale Carnegie, Norvell pushes you to cultivate influential allies while still demonstrating greater beneficence than Machiavelli (who actually had his own sound observations about human nature—that's in our next chapter). To climb the worldly ladder, Norvell advocated using the "law of proximity," which means seeking the company of people who encourage your finest traits, provide good examples to emulate or imitate, do not indulge your lowest habits, and challenge you to match them in mental acumen, not in money.

In his chapter "Awaken the Mental Giant Slumbering Within," Norvell observed how the most retrograde influences in your life are likely to come from "old neighborhood" friends and acquaintances:

They have lived with you for many years and they have been used to the shrinking violet you may have become under the regime of weak, negative thinking of the past. These friends and relatives feel comfortable in the presence of the small ego that fits their concept of your totality of power. When the slumbering mental giant that is within your mind begins to stir restlessly and tries to shake off the chains that bind it to mediocrity, failure, poverty, and ignorance, these people are apt to set up a clamor that will shock the giant back into his somnolent state of immobility and inertia.

I think Norvell must have listened in on my boyhood Thanksgiving dinners back in Queens. Below are ten of my favorite Norvellisms. They may seem obvious, but their depth appears through application. This is often the case with basic-seeming advice. On the surface such guidance may appear elementary; but its power is found only through sustained use.

1. "Most people have a tendency to minimize themselves and their abilities."

2. "To be great, you must dwell in the company of great thoughts and high ideals."

3. "Do not be afraid to ask important people to help you."

4. "Your subconscious mind will give you valuable ideas, but if you do not write them down, they leave suddenly, and it is difficult to recall them again."

5. "Your mind likes definiteness. Give yourself a five-year plan for study, growth, and evolvement."

6. "You must create a need in your life for the things you want."

7. "Determine that you will never use your money for any destructive or degrading act."

8. "Know what you want of life."

9. "You build your sense of self-importance by studying constantly."

10. "No person has ever achieved great heights who was not first inspired by noble emotions and high ideals." (And if you think that you can name an exception, note that the final chapter to most people's lives is not yet written.)

Yes, there are more sophisticated writers of mental therapeutics than Anthony Norvell. You can read the essays of Ralph Waldo Emerson and William James (and you should); you can approach the complex metaphysics of Mary Baker Eddy and Thomas Troward; or you can immerse yourself in the luminous spiritual visions of

Neville Goddard and Ernest Holmes. But there exists in Norvell's work a sapling of all those figures. What's more, Norvell writes with a delightful, infectious simplicity while conveying the basic steps of experimenting with the self-developing agencies of your mind.

I often think of how to reply when asked to recommend a single book on mind power. This could be such a book—it's easily digestible and surprisingly broad in breadth. Norvell's writing is practicality itself.

At times during his long career, Norvell was so prolific—and perhaps needful of the income that came from producing a steady, trendy list of mystical and self-help books—that he stretched his abilities thin. But in the material I've just reviewed, the motivational pioneer was exactly in his element. His insights are often better than who we are today.

Action Step
The Power of Right Relations

Anthony Norvell refers to the "law of proximity"—a valuable building block to an effective life. The law of proximity means using selectivity and decisiveness when seeking relationships, workmates, and friendships. Management guru Peter Drucker (1909–2005) wrote that you should work only with people who are receptive to what you're trying to accomplish. You want colleagues who are supportive, reliable, energetic, and accountable—and who do not make you feel competitive in unhealthy ways.

It is useful to be around people by whom you feel challenged intellectually, by whom you may feel challenged in terms of accomplishment, but never those who make you feel competitive about "keeping up," professionally or personally. You can immediately identify the wrong kind of competitor: they issue subtle putdowns, backhanded compliments, or (sometimes trickily) compare belt notches in matters of money or career. Such relationships are not only depleting, but can push you toward foolish or impulsive behaviors to keep up.

Avoid social events or conversation-circles that make you feel like you need to inflate yourself or showoff your resume. Back in my publishing days, I attended a large dinner of friends and acquaintances where a literary agent said from across the table, "Mitch, tell me what you're working on that's exciting." In private it could be a worthwhile question; in public it felt like a goad to namedropping or preening. I refused, replying that I didn't feel like discussing work. She got the message. If you engage in exchanges that make you feel judged you will often experience depleted energy, the same way that you feel after consuming a large bag of potato chips. It might feel okay at the time but the aftereffects are draining. That feeling should be honored.

Your ground rule: Permit only relationships and conversations that offer mutual and beneficial exchange, and that don't fill you with a sense of unhealthful competitiveness.

You possess a finite amount of time and energy to dedicate to what you're really after. Don't permit depleting social contacts or professional relation-ships to detract from your focus. If you refuse an unwanted engagement or conversation, no one will judge you as not having something to contribute. If anything, you'll be a source of deepened respect and interest. And you'll feel better about yourself.

8

Life Lessons from Machiavelli

"A Prince should show himself a patron of merit."

"Those who come to the Princedom by virtuous paths acquire with difficulty but keep with ease."

"A Prince who is not wise himself cannot be well advised by others."

"The readiest conjecture we can form of the character and sagacity of a Prince is from seeing what sort of men he has about him."

"I do not believe that divisions purposely caused can ever lead to good."

You may be surprised to learn that these are not the say-ings of Buddha. They are aphorisms from diplomat and writer Niccolò Machiavelli's 1532 classic of realpolitik and ruthlessness, *The Prince*.

In today's coarse political and cultural climate, amid the overkill of most online language, Machiavelli's handbook to political brinksmanship looks distinctly noble and pensive by comparison. It warrants rediscov-ery by everyone looking for practical ideas in career, coalitions, and leadership.

For centuries, *The Prince* has been synonymous with tactics of deception and even brutality. "Machia-vellian" is a term for cunning amorality. In the previous chapter, I inveighed against books that endorse morally neutral or unethical methods of personal advancement. How, then, can I justify revisiting *The Prince*, a book considered the urtext of coldblooded attainment?

A fresh look often reveals the unexpected. Machi-avelli imbued *The Prince* with a greater sense of purpose and ethics than is commonly understood. Although Machiavelli unquestionably endorsed absolutist and, at times, ultimate ways of dealing with adversaries, he repeatedly noted that these are last resorts when peace-able means of governance or business prove unworkable. He justified deception or faithlessness only as a defense against the depravity of men, who shift alliances like the winds. This logic by no means approaches the moral-ity of Christ's dictum to be as "wise as serpents and harmless as doves," but it belies the general notion of Machiavelli as a one-dimensional schemer.

Moreover, the author emphasizes rewarding merit (not family, sycophants, or hacks); leaving the public to its own devices as much as possible (the essential ingredient, he writes, to developing culture and economy); trusting subjects enough to allow them to bear arms—and even arming them yourself if confident in their loyalty (as a good leader should be); surrounding oneself with wise counselors (the true measure of a ruler's ability); rejecting and not exploiting civic divisions (which weaken the whole nation); and striving to ensure the public's general satisfaction.

One of the most striking parts of the book for me is when Machiavelli expounds on the best kind of intellect for an adviser, minister—or, in today's terms, an executive. I am quoting from the 1910 translation of Renaissance scholar N.H. Thomson:

> There are three scales of intelligence, one which understands by itself, a second which understands what it is shown by others, and a third, which understands neither by itself nor by the showing of others, the first of which is most excellent, the second good, but the third worthless.

This has always been my favorite passage of Machiavelli's, and I challenge you to consider what place you have earned on its scale.

Some contemporary critics suggest that *The Prince* is actually a satire of monarchy: that under the guise of writing a guide to bare-knuckled maneuvering, Machiavelli instead lampoons the actions of absolute rulers and covertly calls for more civic forms of rulership. I think this assessment stretches matters. But it would be equally wrong to conclude that Machiavelli was a narrow-eyed courtier bent solely on reducing others. On balance, Machiavelli was a pragmatic tutor interested in promoting the unity, stability and integrity of nation states, chiefly his own Italy, in a Europe that lacked cohesive civics and reliable international treaties. His harsher ideas were then considered acceptable quivers in the bow of statecraft; you will also see his efforts to leaven them with insights about the vicissitudes of human nature, fate and virtue.

Although Machiavelli was considered a master of opportunistically shaping and breaking alliances, he inveighed against divisiveness and racial animus. He also admired excellence in government—and the leader who fostered it:

> The choice of Ministers is a matter of no small moment to a Prince. Whether they shall be good or not depends on his prudence, so that the readiest conjecture we can form of the character and sagacity of a Prince is from seeing what sort of men he has about him. When they are at once capable and faithful, we may always account him wise, since he has known to recognize their merit and to retain their fidelity. But if they be otherwise, we must pronounce unfavorably of him, since he has committed a first fault in making this selection.

Lastly, Machiavelli believed that the best rulers hold power not by sneakiness but intelligence, tough-mindedness, and refinement through personal trial:

"They who come to the Princedom . . . by virtuous paths, acquire with difficulty, but keep with ease."

I advise experiencing *The Prince* through the filter of your own ethical standards and inner truths; sifting among its practical lessons; taking in its tough observations about human weaknesses; and using it as a guide to the realities—and foibles—of human events.

I believe that leaders in business, activism, or government who read *The Prince* today will discover subtleties that are missing from our culture's power-at-any-cost ethos.

Action Step
Wisdom for Warriors

I do not mean to imply here or in the previous chapter that seeking and attaining success does not sometimes involve friction, conflict, or overcoming foes. Sometimes it is necessary to push back resistance. Since its first creditable English translation in 1910, the Chinese martial text *The Art of War* has enthralled Westerners with what it teaches about facing down adversity with effectiveness and startling suddenness. The book is a mainstay among contemporary martial artists, soldiers, strategists, and perceptive businesspeople.

This is a surprising posterity for a work of ancient warfare estimated to be written around 500 BC by Zhou dynasty general Sun Tzu, an honorific title meaning "Master Sun." Very little is known about Sun Tzu other than a historical consensus that such a figure actually existed as a commander in the dynastic emperor's army. What can an ancient field guide teach today's creative-mind seekers?

The Art of War returns us to insights into life and its inevitable conflicts that we may have once understood intuitively but lost in superfluous and speculative analysis, another of life's inevitabilities. Author Sun Tzu teaches adhering to the natural landscape, blending with the curvature and qualities of one's surroundings, and locating your place in the organic order of things. Within the Vedic tradition this is sometimes called dharma. As the great Hermetic dictum put it: "As above, so below."

Sun Tzu's central idea is that the greatest warrior prevails without ever fighting. If a seeker has observed conditions, deciphered his foe or obstacle, and diligently prepared and marshaled his forces, the ideal is to overwhelm your opposition without shooting a single arrow. "Supreme excellence," Sun Tzu writes, "consists in breaking the enemy's resistance without fighting." (I am quoting from the 1910 English translation by British sinologist Lionel Giles.)

After you overcome obstacles, you must quickly return to peace and equilibrium. "In war then," the master writes, "let your object be victory, not lengthy campaigns." Sun Tzu warns against protracted operations: "There is no instance of a country having benefited from prolonged warfare."

Rather than seek glory, Sun Tzu counsels that the excellent martial artist practice subtlety, inscrutability, watchfulness, and flexibility. Be like water, he writes, dwelling unnoticed at the lowest depths and then striking with overwhelming force, the way a torrent of water rushes downhill. Be patient, look for your foe's weakness, and then strike with overwhelming force.

If I had to put *The Art of War* into a nutshell, I would use this one of Sun Tzu's maxims: "Let your plans be dark and impenetrable as night, and when you move, fall like a thunderbolt."

In a sense, *The Art of War* is about unlearning the complexities of life and returning to the patterns of nature, much like Ralph Waldo Emerson and Henry David Thoreau prescribed. It returns us to what is simple, powerful, and true.

9

Real Leadership

In *The Law of Success*, Napoleon Hill defined leadership simply as initiative:

> *Leadership* is essential for the attainment of *Success*, and *Initiative* is the very foundation upon which this necessary quality of *Leadership* is built. *Initiative* is as essential to success as a hub is essential to a wagon wheel. And what is *Initiative*? It is that exceedingly rare quality that prompts—nay, impels—a person to do that which ought to be done without being told to do it ... One of the peculiarities of *Leadership* is the fact that it is never found in those who have not acquired the *habit* of taking the initiative. Leadership is something that you must invite yourself into; it will never thrust itself upon you.

My rules for leadership are simple, and relate closely to Hill's: I believe that a real leader should never ask those who report to him to do anything that he wouldn't be willing to do himself. Also, a good leader should be able to take over a task himself—no matter how apparently menial—and should know how to do it. A leader who cannot ship a package or clean a toilet, or is unwilling to, is not a leader. "A great man is always willing to be little," Ralph Waldo Emerson wrote in his essay *Compensation*.

People have no right to "wait" for leadership to be granted to them; they establish it by their personal effectiveness.

All of this came home to me at a stage in my career when I was stripped of all assistance and left to do things for myself that I normally handed off to another. It meant ordering paperclips, taking random phone calls, and performing clerical tasks. At first my pride was wounded, and I was unsure of how to proceed. I soon learned a lesson in leadership that has remained with me ever since: a true leader never places him or herself above any task. I was reminded of the words of Napoleon Bonaparte, as recorded by Ralph Waldo Emerson in his 1860 essay *Success*. This is really a message of self-sufficiency:

> "There is nothing in war," said Napoleon, "which I cannot do by my own hands. If there is nobody to make gunpowder, I can manufacture it. The gun-carriages I know how to construct. If it is necessary to make cannons at the forge, I can make them. The details of working them in battle, if it is necessary to teach, I shall teach

them. In administration, it is I alone who have arranged the finances, as you know."

I recognize that you may already be doing all of these things, but the path of leadership, or the recognition of your natural leadership, seems blocked. All of us sometimes find ourselves within organizations, military units, or workplaces where the path to leadership is closed off, occupied, or jealously guarded. Or, if you are an artist or entrepreneur your leadership may depend upon receiving funding to start your project and assume command. In such cases, you may feel like Napoleon Bonaparte when he was exiled on the island of Saint Helena. I've been there.

In these predicaments make a careful study of the "Law of Cycles" in the upcoming chapter on luck. Sometimes you must simply hone your abilities and stand your ground with dignity and resolve until your opportunity arrives. It will arrive in one form or another. The Wheel of Fortune is ever turning and spares no one, for good or ill. While you are waiting, do exactly what the actor, martial artist, musician, or commando does: *train, train, train*. You will be all-the-more ready to seize the reins of action when they fall to you.

I also believe that a real leader should tell the truth. This includes taking responsibility publicly when things go wrong, and not passing off the blame, subtly or otherwise, to a subordinate, or dodging questions. Some who hold positions of leadership manage to be out of the room or conveniently miss a meeting or conference call when a dicey issue arises. This may work in the short term but it will never make someone authoritative in the truest sense.

This brings me to my final point: The influence of a real leader should outlast his or her title or office. Because, like everything in life, a title and its privileges will suddenly or eventually get taken away. Your works alone will remain. And in that legacy appears the one true measure of leadership.

Action Step
Do You *Want* to Lead?

Many of us think we want to be boss. But, in actuality, sometimes we really don't want to be the one in charge. Our wish for leadership or influence may be best expressed through a different path than the conventional one.

For a long time, I thought I wanted to lead inside a media organization. But after years, I realized that I was more comfortable pursuing my own writing and speaking, and doing much of my work in private and then presenting it before an audience. I didn't want to dedicate my day to solving other people's problems. I had a friend who was the CEO of a mid-sized industrial company in the Midwest; he told me that when you're CEO you get more pay and deference but you belong to everyone else. Your door, in effect, is constantly open to people bringing you their predicaments, personal and otherwise. He had no one to turn to, but everyone wanted to turn to him.

It took me a while to realize that, like my CEO friend, I didn't really want that, and probably wasn't well suited to it.

I derive greater satisfaction from writing an article, narrating a book, or delivering a talk than I do from convening a meeting, producing a quarterly budget, or supervising someone else's work. I felt much more relaxed when I finally came to terms with that.

At the same time, there *is* a kind of leadership in what I do. Writing and speaking, if done well, can make you a thought leader. People come to you with their sincere questions. This entails a great deal of responsibility. Something I always try to remember, and counsel others, is to watch out for a somewhat dodgy kind of theater that can grow out of playing the role of thought leader. I know firsthand what it's like to sit across a table from someone who sees me as "the man with the plan," and wants me to provide the answers to problems. This kind of dynamic elevates the person receiving the question, and imbues him or her with more authority than may be deserved. Entire relationships—with ministers, teachers, therapists, or group leaders—can develop this way, and remain in place for years. These relationships can end in disappointment when the questioner realizes that the authority figure is no more developed or capable of applying wisdom in his or her private life than the questioner. When this awareness dawns, feelings of betrayal or anger can arise, especially if the figure of authority has flaunted his or her expertise.

I am not a teacher. I am a seeker. I chronicle metaphysical experience in history and practice. My own act of seeking is reflected in my topics.

Nearly everything that I write and speak about represents an area of exploration and inquiry for me personally. I sometimes make mistakes or overstate something; later I may refine and restate an idea differently. This is the price of my public-private search. But one thing that I always endeavor to bring is transparency.

A journalist friend once wryly noted that life must be difficult for motivational or positive-mind teachers. They must always be "on." Of course, being "on" is often just an act. In nearly thirty years in spiritual publishing, I have never once met a writer or teacher who I believed demonstrated congruity between his or her public and private life. Maybe it's an unfair standard, but it is reasonable to ask whether someone is living his or her own teachings. Hence, I try to be frank with you throughout this book about my own fitful efforts—including in my later chapter about identifying a definite chief *weakness*. I owe you, as the reader, bluntness in my testimony. If I am any kind of leader (and, again, I see myself more as a seeker) that alone is where it comes from.

Ask yourself: Do you *want* to be a traditional leader? Or do you seek a different kind of expression? Leadership, in its broadest iteration, can be experienced in a wide range of ways. Never settle for the conventional role of leader if that's not what you truly want.

10

The 10 Rules of Good Luck

Napoleon Hill's system is one of mental preparation, effective strategy, and organized planning—not of blind luck. Yet the question of nurturing favorable circumstances in no way chafes against Hill's outlook. Indeed, the question of "good luck" is intriguing, and even mysterious.

A neurosurgeon once told me never to take notions of luck lightly. "I've seen patients live or die on an operating table based on what we call luck," he said. The surgeon confided that he took "lucky feelings" and signs seriously. He went as far as rescheduling operations if he got a sense or portent that something was amiss.

Yet we have difficulty saying what luck really is. Good or bad luck could be seen as merely accidental. But is anything truly accidental when the law of cause-and-effect is detectable behind every event, even if only after the fact? Seen in a certain way, I believe that we are capable of cultivating or improving our luck. Obviously no one can control the myriad factors behind each occurrence. Yet I have observed that certain practices and habits regularly improve luck or, put another way, sway circumstances in one's favor. This is true even if the recipient is unaware of what's occurring. Hence, the personal factors that trigger good luck should always be respected.

A famous actor once confided his secret to success: "Determine the things that make you lucky, and then do more of them." Implicit in his statement is the belief that certain identifiable actions, practices, and environments are, by their nature, lucky. I not only embrace that perspective but I believe that "luck factors" can be distilled into general rules that are applicable to nearly anyone's life.

Filmmaker David Lynch recalled that when he attended art school in Philadelphia he wasn't interested in making movies but in painting. Yet he began to see film as a kind of "moving painting," and his interests gradually shifted in that direction. At a certain point he had to decide which medium to commit to. How do you know where to direct your energies? "Watch for those green lights," he said. Look for where you're getting the most encouragement, satisfaction, and opportunities. Simple as it may sound, not everyone's "green lights" are immediately evident. Sometimes you may not feel that you're getting *any*. The factors I am about to review will not only help you identify your green lights, but will also help you position yourself in the places where they occur.

I approach the topic of luck not as a statistician—although laws of odds and statistics play a part in it—but rather as a media veteran who has observed people across a wide range of fields rise, fall, or undergo inertia based on the 10 Rules of Good Luck that I explore below. Talent and cognition surely matter; but, again, I have observed that pivotal events in people's careers, and sometimes over the arc of their entire adulthoods, result from the presence or absence of the practices and disciplines I consider here. If followed, these practices place capable people into the positive current of destiny, or the flow of good luck.

Rule I: Cultivate Chemistry

Your most personal decision in life, observed Italian novelist Ignacio Silone, is "the choice of comrades." The company you select plays a tremendous part not only in the values you live out but also in the opportunities you experience and the nature of what you do with them.

In 2010, this topic arose when rock performer Mick Jagger spoke to interviewer Larry King:

> KING: How do you account for the longevity of the Stones as a success?

> JAGGER: Well, I think the Stones are very lucky. You always need a lot of luck. And I think they were in the right place at the right time. And when we work, we work very hard. So I think you need all those things. You

know, there's no good just being hardworking because lots of people are hardworking. But you've got to be hardworking, on your game, and be lucky...

KING: ... Don't eliminate the word 'luck.'

JAGGER: No, I'm not eliminating luck... whatever your way of life, if you get to be very successful there is usually some point where you just happen to be lucky.

One of the factors that Jagger did not mention, at least specifically, is the luck of *good chemistry*. Part of the Rolling Stones' success is that they gelled extraordinarily well as musicians, writers, and performers, as well as in personal image and looks. (This was also thanks to the vision of founding member Brian Jones (1942–1969) who receives insufficient credit.) The Stones have functioned with remarkable posterity as a group. By contrast, Jagger, a virtuoso performer and brilliant businessman, actually has a spotty record with his solo albums, despite enormous resources, fame, and talent placed behind them. His chemistry with the Rolling Stones is singular; it cannot be duplicated in other parts of his career.

Take a personal cue from this. Scan your life for areas of charmed relations and special chemistry—and preserve them. Good partnerships, whether in art, commerce, or intimate life, are rare and valuable. They are worth defending.

Years ago, I had a boss whom I both loved and, at times, felt deep frustration with. I am sure he felt the same toward me. Whenever I was tempted to leave my workplace and go it alone, I reflected on our long and extraordinary partnership, and the success it had produced. I stayed put. We possessed similar tastes, sympathies, and temperaments. Our weaknesses and strengths complemented one another's. We had a genuinely good time working together. Whatever the occasional frustrations, our joint success was truly notable. We maintained our partnership for nearly twenty years, and continue to collaborate today. I view this relationship, and the chemistry inherent in it, as one of the key sources of my success.

Never take for granted the power of relationship and collaboration. Things that you attribute to your talents alone may, in reality, be due to the intangible but vital chemistry that arises from the complementary efforts, well-balanced weaknesses and strengths, personal affinities, and shared visions that you have with a partner, investor, collaborator, or workmate. *Good chemistry is good luck.* Seek it out. Scan your life for it. And when you find good chemistry, or if you already possess it, value and maintain it.

Rule II: Prepared Minds Win

In 1854 the pioneering scientist and germ theorist Louis Pasteur said in a lecture at the University of Lille in Northern France: "In the fields of observation chance favors only the prepared mind." This statement has been popularly—and, I think, accurately—shortened into: "Chance favors the prepared mind." If you wish to be lucky, make this your personal motto.

Chance opportunities are useful only to those who are *prepared* for them—and the greater the preparation, the more fully you will be able to take advantage when they arrive. Preparation heightens all of the other chance factors around you; it ensures that you'll be in the right mental state to notice, receive, and profit from opportunities.

By preparation, I do not mean using Google to peer into the lives of job interviewers or coworkers, a practice I discourage. I mean preparation of *yourself*. You should know of, and be reasonably versed in, every aspect of your field, even as you focus on a niche or specialty within it. Be aware of current technology and developments in your field and workspace. Be well rounded about overall practices and trends. And, above all, be an absolute expert within your specific area of focus—and be sure you have one. Practice your craft as a martial artist repeatedly runs a routine to the point where it becomes a part of his or her bodily knowledge.

Joseph Murphy emphasized this point in *The Power of Your Subconscious Mind*:

> If a young man chooses chemistry as his profession, he should concentrate on one of the many branches in this field. He should give all of his time and attention to his chosen specialty. He should become sufficiently enthusiastic to try to know all there is available about his field; if possible, he should know more than anyone else. The young man should become ardently interested in his work and should desire to serve the world.

Motivational writer Dale Carnegie provided an interesting case in point. Carnegie began his career in the early-twentieth century as a teacher of public speaking. A former actor, the young teacher grasped that public speaking was becoming a vital skill for businesspeople in the years following World War I. When preparing for a talk or pitch, Carnegie observed that you should amass so much material that you discard ninety-percent of it when actually speaking. The very fact of your preparation gives you the confidence and power to speak without notes, and to deliver a relaxed, enthusiastic, and freestyle performance.

Carnegie's formula is a recipe for good outcomes in all areas of life. Once you are justifiably confident and expert in a task or project, you can watch, listen, intuit, and become cognizant of important cues. Ardent preparation makes you persuasive. Your actions become natural and effortless. You can pivot. You exude confidence. You gain a childlike enthusiasm. And, as Pasteur alluded, things have a way of *reaching you*, or at least of reaching your attention, which would otherwise go unnoticed.

Preparation allows you to bend the unexpected to your advantage. I once met former Vermont governor and Democratic presidential candidate Howard Dean while he was riding alone on the New York City subways. I said hello and he could not have been friendlier. ("It's the only way to get around New York," he said.) Dean called Pasteur's expression, "chance favors the prepared mind," his personal motto. Dean repeated it to colleagues, campaign workers, and political collaborators, especially when he was chair of the Democratic

National Committee. As chair, Dean insisted that the Democratic Party adopt a "50-state strategy," that is, strengthening its presence and ground operation in even those states where Democrats historically lost. If the political tide were to turn, or if a seemingly predictable race got upended, he reasoned, the more prepared party would win.

This is a universally applicable principle. When opportunities appear in your path, such as a job opening, an audition, a call to make a presentation on the fly at a conference, or even being seated next to your boss on an airplane, the prepared person will be able to seize the moment. Always remember: *Luck favors the prepared mind.*

Rule III: Profit from the Law of Cycles

If you've ever shuffled through a deck of Tarot cards you've probably noticed the beguiling image called the Wheel of Fortune. It displays animals, sometimes of a mythical nature, sometimes of a recognizable one, rising and falling on a rotating wheel. It is an archetypal image in the Western mind.

The Wheel of Fortune captures an important principle about the fundamentally cyclical nature of life. This principle harbors a universal truth that can come to your rescue.

In essence, all of life is subject to a Law of Cycles. This principle dictates that events within and without you flow like the seasons or the tides. The ancient Hermeticists and nineteenth-century Transcendentalists both understood that if you want to glean the laws under which we live—including those laws that govern your psyche and your daily existence—you should study the cycles and revolutions of nature. As go the seasons, tides, and circuit-like motions of the cosmos, so go our lives. "As above, so below," taught the Hermetic work called the Emerald Tablet.

What can this teach you about daily living? The revolutions of the Wheel of Fortune tell you to purposefully *stand in your place*. If you are earnestly and diligently working, training, drilling, rehearsing, preparing, and doing your labor, the Wheel of Fortune dictates that, eventually and inevitably, the cyclical law of rise and fall will reach you directly where you are standing. In time, this law will lift your fortunes in their desired direction. "An assumption," wrote mystic Neville Goddard, "though false, if persisted in, will eventually harden into fact."

Of course, reversals are also part of this law. Any gambler or statistician can tell you about "runs of luck." Runs always reverse. So be careful. The flipping of a two-sided object must eventually even out, for good or ill, depending upon your perspective. Three good hits in a row presage a near-certain reversal.

But there is a way of cultivating the Law of Cycles for your benefit. People often complain that their schools or workplaces are not meritocracies; that life just isn't fair. And they are right—to a point. I have personally, and sometimes frustratingly, witnessed feckless or mediocre people survive or even thrive in competitive situations. But this happens only if they manage to stick around long enough. The Law of Cycles eventually works in their favor. It is a peculiar feature of life, and particularly of career, art, and culture, that failures are often forgotten in the midst of success. In terms of perception, one success can outweigh or mitigate a lot of failures. This is because people sense, without fully knowing why, that a success will strike again. They want to be there when it does. This gives a hint of how persistence can help you "outsmart" the Law of Cycles.

Consider: If a mediocre person, by just sticking around, can experience success in unexpected (though lawful) hours, imagine how much greater a success you can personally experience if you persevere as a figure of excellence. A truly prepared and driven person is vastly more primed to reap the fruits of an upturn in the Law of Cycles than a merely mediocre one. Live by this.

Although downturns are equally inevitable, they are more often forgotten. Successes linger. This is why an artist, entrepreneur, campaign strategist, or battle-field commander can build his or her reputation on a single success, no matter how many reversals preceded or followed it. It happened to Winston Churchill, albeit on an epic scale. Churchill made horrendous military errors in World War I in Turkey; his missteps tragically claimed the lives of literally tens of thousands of Allied soldiers. Later considered inept in domestic politics, the wartime leader was actually voted out of office immediately following World War II. But Churchill's success as the desperately needed hero of World War II lingers. And always will.

On a more humdrum note, the same thing happens to an apathetic coworker in the accounting department who dines out year after year on having once saved the company money (and who may also have an indulgent boss). Everyone wonders: how does he survive on the job? The fact is, one success can be sustaining.

As an archetypal image, the Wheel of Fortune reminds us of life's lawful inevitabilities, and the imperative to prepare for them. The message is: remain on course; or, if things are going beautifully, prepare for winter. But one thing the card doesn't reveal, at least explicitly, is that the purposeful and aware individual can "ride" these cycles, knowing that the apex will always again come into sight.

This is why Churchill told a group of boarding school students at his alma mater Harrow in 1941: "Never give in, never give in, never, never, never, never—in nothing, great or small, large or petty—never give in except to convictions of honor and good sense. Never yield to force; never yield to the apparently overwhelming might of the enemy."

This might sound like typical bluster, but the British leader recognized a greater truth to which he alluded in the same speech: "You cannot tell from appearances how things will go." This is because appearances, like everything else in nature and in life, are constantly and lawfully changing.

Understand that, and you will have gleaned a core part of the wisdom of the Law of Cycles—and the deeper meaning behind the benefits of intelligent persistence.

Rule IV: Failure Is Lucky

To say "failure is lucky" isn't some cloying bromide. Napoleon Hill insisted that the motivated person should never see failure as final but rather as a temporary set-back. From personal experience, I strongly believe this is true. I can think of numerous times in my life when an apparent failure was lucky for either one of two reasons:

1) Because it protected me from a job, course of action, or relationship for which I was unsuited. Other times a failure protected me from an environment that may have been on the brink of bad luck. For example, I once lost the chance of leading a publishing company, which actually turned out to be perched on financial quicksand and soon descended into near-bankruptcy and mass layoffs. I did not want to be there to preside over a funeral. I also lost a job bid at a national magazine—but, again, the outcome was lucky. It was a political magazine whose celebrity editor (and a good man) died in a flight accident, which plunged his once-ascendant magazine into discord and dissolution. The "dream job" would have been a disaster. I mourn this man's passing. But I feel relieved I was never on the scene.

2) Other times, failures or setbacks lit a fire within me by illuminating my own weaknesses and missteps, which drove me to more intelligent forms of striving and the long-term realization of cherished aims. That leads to my story immediately below.

I want to share with you a painful but ultimately helpful episode in my professional life. I offer this not because I want to be morbidly self-disclosing but because I feel that I owe you an honest reckoning of how these principles have played out for me personally. When I was writing my first book in 2009, I agreed to provide a piece of the book-in-progress to a small, independent metaphysical magazine. They gratefully published it—but when the print magazine reached my home I discovered that the piece, which I felt that I provided them as a favor and which was frankly of a higher quality than their standard fare, was buried deep inside and not mentioned on the cover. It looked like filler.

This was in no way intended as a slight, but nonetheless I felt dejected—as though my work wasn't prized in the very place that it should have been. Rather than get depressed, however, I vowed as I held that magazine in my hands that I would never again write for venues that didn't show reciprocity—and I would seek out bigger and better venues. In the years immediately ahead, my byline appeared in places including the *New York Times, Washington Post, Wall Street Journal, Time, Politico,* and other major national media. My articles were on the same kinds of esoteric subjects I had written about up until then for smaller magazines. I didn't compromise topic, ideals, or quality. That, too, was a victory.

My perception of poor recognition drove me to heights that I might not otherwise have reached. What felt like a setback became a springboard. It was, in a sense, a lucky failure—from which mature victories grew.

I must also note that too much success, too soon, can be self-destructive. I have witnessed very talented authors and media figures get suddenly catapulted to national recognition and near-celebrity. I have seen these things seriously strain their relationships and work habits. Struggle had served them better than arrival. Peaking at a young age can bring similar disadvantage. In addition to questions of emotional preparation, problems arise because someone's run of luck arrives early, lawfully reverses, and he or she often spends decades trying to regain past glories. At one point in my publishing career, I noticed that nearly every quality writer with whom I worked, who produced books of depth and posterity, was already in middle age. The solidity of their output may be attributable to the amassing of experience, but I believe it was also because these writers never took their success for granted.

Rule V: "No" Is Not Final

An entrepreneur I admire was attempting to meet with a colleague he knew through mutual friends. But the colleague kept putting him off. Finally, the two did get together—and enjoyed each other's company. My friend asked his once-hesitant companion why he had resisted meeting him.

"Well," the other man said, "you're someone who has a reputation for not taking no for an answer." He considered my friend hard-charging and wasn't sure he wanted to get together.

My friend replied pensively: "You're right. I don't take no for an answer. But it's because conditions can change, and then the answer changes."

Always remember that: *Conditions can change, and then the answer changes.*

This doesn't mean being a noodge or badgering people. That will get you nowhere. It means keeping open the lines of communication and keeping relationships healthy so that you can always re-approach someone. Essayist Elbert Hubbard wrote in his "Credo" in 1912: "I believe that when I part with you I must do it in such a way that when you see me again you will be glad—and so will I." Don't undervalue that sentiment. Conditions in business, and other facets of life, change or reverse all the time. This is natural law. If you have the capacity to re-approach people, and the presence of mind to do so, you can take advantage of these natural changes. So long as you've maintained sound relations, never feel hesitant or embarrassed about knocking on someone's door a second, third, or even fourth time. A music executive once told me: "Be a pest but be a *nice* pest."

I've hit dry spells with assignment editors at magazines and newspapers only to find that after I went away for a time and then returned they became newly receptive to my pitches, possibly because of a change in the news cycle or some other factor that made my ideas more relevant.

I know a successful movie producer who has a talent for not taking no. He is unerringly friendly to nearly everyone. He offends no one. And he knows when to step away for a while. Hence, he is always capable of revisiting plans, pitches, and relationships.

When conditions shift in your favor, and someone substitutes a yes for a no, accept your good fortune gladly—and never remind someone of his or her previous refusals. You alone will know the mechanics behind the welcome reversal.

Rule VI: Never Confuse Enthusiasm with Optimism

Philosopher Ralph Waldo Emerson famously wrote, "Nothing great was ever achieved without enthusiasm." This is a valuable truth. Enthusiasm is not only infectious but it drives you to perform at your highest. Without it every task is menial. But it is vital never to confuse enthusiasm with blind optimism. Indeed, enthusiasm coupled with a *watchful wariness* is a highly potent combination.

I know a lucky minority of people who continually check and recheck their work. They do so well past the point where the average person would stop. Sometimes they are teased by colleagues who tell them that they ought to relax, take it slower, and not take life so seriously. They are sometimes called obsessive, worrywarts, or Type-A personalities. Well, the ones who persistently recheck their work are often life's winners. When surprise glitches occur—and they will—such people catch them before harm is done. This has happened to me.

In the summer of 2003, *Science of Mind* magazine handed me the dream assignment of interviewing all-star pitcher Barry Zito. Barry used mind-metaphysics as part of his training regimen. His major inspirations included Ernest Holmes and Neville Goddard. Landing this interview was a major "get" for the magazine, and its editors brought it to me as someone they felt they could trust. I was determined not to let them down. The resulting article, "Barry's Way," became a major springboard to my writing career. But the whole thing was almost derailed—and I have never written about it before. Due to a minor audio glitch, I nearly blew the interview. *Nearly.* I didn't blow it because I was wary enough to recheck my recording equipment.

As it happens, the cassette recorder I was using to tape my phone interview was, for whatever reason, switched to an odd function that would have muted Barry's end of the conversation. But this wasn't detectable until you were recording live. Had the function been left that way, the whole encounter would've been lost. I had already tested my record function before the interview. It worked fine. But I decided, past what might have seemed necessary, to record a test call. When I did, I discovered the problem. It was just a couple of minutes before I was scheduled to speak with Barry. I have sometimes wondered how my life might be different today if I hadn't been healthfully wary enough to avert this serious accident, simply because I cared enough to recheck my tech under live conditions.

It is the same with logistics, names, spellings, facts, numbers, and arithmetic. You will never regret honoring that creeping feeling that *something* may be off. Assuming the worst and rechecking your work will, at one time or another (and it has happened to me more than once), save an assignment, presentation, legal matter, job interview, or exam.

Let others leave work early and line up at the bar. You remain behind and recheck your work. *Luck favors the pessimistic enthusiast.*

Rule VII: Humiliate No One

It is a rule of human nature that when you insult or disrespect someone you will forget about it a lot sooner than the injured party will. In fact, when you publicly humiliate someone—in a meeting, online, or at an event—that person literally *never* forgets it. Emotions form memories. That is a key to human nature. Another key holds that people will, sometimes at an unexpected moment, strike back if the chance arises.

Years ago there was a politically ambitious prosecutor in New York City who aspired to run for mayor. Fairly or not, she had developed a reputation for putting down colleagues and subordinates. One day, she arrived late to a public meeting, which had begun in her absence. Incensed at the perceived slight, she put a stop to the meeting and insisted that it be started over in her presence. Eyes rolled. Not long after, someone leaked a story to the city tabloids about supposed excesses in her spending on office furniture. The media scandal blunted her political career.

I have no idea who made the disclosure, or whether it was true. But I wasn't surprised to see it in the headlines of a tabloid. My assumption is that her coworkers, nursing bruised egos, decided, rightly or not, to seize upon the opportunity to strike back. The same thing happened to Minnesota Senator Amy Klobuchar in the early stages of the 2020 Democratic presidential primaries. News articles ran sometimes-anonymous accounts of how severe a boss the candidate could be. Fairly or not, the news coverage proved politically embarrassing.

It is not only ethically wrong to wound another's self-respect, but you have no way of knowing the moment when such a score will be settled. Even if you think you can afford to disrespect a subordinate or gopher, you are wrong. And not for moral reasons alone (although those are enough). That person may be privy to material that can one day inconvenience or embarrass you.

This same rule holds true on social media, and even in supposedly private emails or texts. Rid yourself of the notion that anything is truly private. Routine emails and texts get shared all the time. And we've all had—or will have—the experience of mistakenly hitting "reply all," or copying an unintended party, on a sensitive message—maybe even the party you're talking about. I know three people whose jobs were lost and lives upended due to innocent errors like that. Before you hit "send," ask yourself if you've written anything that would embarrass or harm you if it got read in public. A media executive once told her staff never to put anything in an email that you wouldn't want read aloud in a court of law.

The temptation to be snarky and sarcastic on social media can be nearly irresistible. People feel disinhibited by the personal remove or perceived anonymity. But always remember that online comments are forever, even if erased. User anonymity may afford some protection but I have my doubts. And, believe me, when you insult someone online the wounded party remembers it—always. If you do happen to flame someone or wound his or her feelings, whether online, at work, or in public, sometimes in a moment of anger or stress, then *apologize*. And do so sincerely.

My one basic rule is that you shouldn't post, email, or text anything that you wouldn't be willing to say aloud to someone's face. Abiding by that practice could one day save your job, your relationships, and your peace of mind.

Rule VIII: Recognize Others

This rule builds on the one we just considered. Rather than merely avoiding offense, you should actively and sincerely build people up—not in a cloying manner but when properly due. Get in the habit of thanking people and recognizing their legitimate contribution to a project. And if you're an employer or the purchaser of a service, do so in cold, hard cash when the occasion calls for it.

Saying thank you is not just courtesy. By recognizing other people—privately, publicly, and, when appropriate, in remuneration—you allow them to feel that they benefit from your success, and you give them a stake in its continuance.

William James observed in a letter in 1896: "The deepest principle of Human Nature is the craving to be appreciated." People hunger to be seen. Never underestimate the power of recognition. Giving it is usually free, and it brings immense returns. Those who feel that you have recognized them will endeavor to find a lost or late check, to put you first on a list, and to make sure your package goes out after the office closes.

The opposite also holds true. If you fail to properly recognize people they won't necessarily hinder your work, but they will feel apathy toward it. I have been thanked innumerable times, and I have truly appreciated it. But, in full disclosure, I must confess that I more keenly recollect those times when I have not been appropriately thanked. Perhaps you do, too. It is a fissure in human nature that we are more likely to recall when expectations are unfulfilled. I don't know why—it might have something to do with a primal need for safety, or childhood conflicts.

Whatever the case, always remember that "invisible helpers" appear, or not, based on whether we have thanked and recognized them. Recognizing people is homage to the gods of luck.

In matters of money, you can and should remunerate valuable people and service providers. Even if you cannot offer them extra pay or bonuses, you can accrue similar benefit by *paying people quickly*. I cannot overstate the goodwill engendered by paying a contractor, employee, artist, or vendor quickly—preferably upon completion of a task.

Quick pay often means as much, or more, than the sum itself. I know a publisher who pays people by electronic transfer within twenty-four to forty-eight hours after delivery. This builds tremendous loyalty and appreciation. By contrast, I have personal experience with New Age and spiritual centers that drag their feet on paying even modest sums to speakers and workshop facilitators. I will not work for such places again.

You demonstrate that you value someone's work not only in cash but also in *how you deliver it*. Speed is free. Its dividends are invaluable.

Rule IX: Show Up

Are you reliable? A large part of what makes someone reliable is the simple but vital act of showing up, and showing up on time, for commitments, both social and work-related. You have no idea how fully other people notice this and judge you by it. What's more, showing up puts you into the flow of good luck.

In today's culture, people are too at ease bailing on commitments, whether social or work-related, for nearly any reason. Busyness is not a sufficient excuse (at least not usually). The need to run an errand is not a sufficient excuse. Nor is feeling a bit under-the-weather or having a cold, depending on the nature of the commitment. We as a culture are, I believe, too self-coddling. We deem things urgent that are merely passing. A philosopher friend puts it this way: "The only real emergency is a medical emergency."

Keeping your engagements and being on time not only marks you for reliability but something more: important and often-fortuitous things happen to those who place themselves within the flow of life. Chance encounters, of the most unexpected variety, can open you to a new job or give you the break for which you are searching. I am not suggesting that you should go to every engagement with the anxious expectation that you'll meet someone vital; but odds are that one day it *will* occur.

One night in New York a close friend was hosting a party. I attended but felt bored and out of sorts. I was planning to leave early. But out of loyalty to my friend I changed my mind. He wanted me there, and I decided to stick around. About 45 minutes later a woman showed up who became my future wife. We had two children together. This is how strangely life can work. If I had left I would not have met a vital, central person in my life. Mind you, I wasn't sticking around for personal gain. I was doing it to honor my friend. But honoring an obligation to another, and hence staying in the flow of life, placed me in the path of a positive, life-altering experience. *Fate shines on those whom it can reach.*

Here is a story of a slightly different tenor. It may seem extreme but consider it carefully. One night following a speaking event at a photography museum, I was hanging around backstage with a group of experienced news photographers. These people had distinguished themselves in the sharp-elbowed world of photojournalism. As it happened, many of them had known each other when they were younger and working as interns at *Time* magazine. As the night went on, the photographers began trading "war stories." To laughter all around, one recounted when he was tasked with bringing important film from a news event across town to *Time*'s offices, then in Midtown Manhattan. On the way, he got into a car accident, which wasn't grave but was serious enough so that an ambulance was called and paramedics removed him from his car.

When the paramedics asked how he felt, he started explaining in halting terms that he needed to get this film across town. The group of photographers laughed at what could be seen as an absurd mismatch of priorities. Since no one was hurt, it was the kind of story that one could look back on and laugh. *But consider how few people would demonstrate the kind of indestructible dedication that the speaker did.* (And the film did get there.) Certainly you could say that the young photographer had gone too far, or that he displayed an unhealthy one-sided devotion to his job. But, personally, I don't think so. Wouldn't you want your surgeon, nurse, pilot, or someone in law enforcement to demonstrate that degree of dedication? If you were a coach, wouldn't you want that from your players? Maybe the example sounds extreme. But it highlights the character of people who distinguish themselves—and who *honor commitments*. Every successful photographer that night had a similar story or attitude. Learn from it. Luck favors the intrepid.

Rule X: Act Quickly

Napoleon Hill dedicated a full chapter of *Think and Grow Rich* to the power of decisiveness. He observed how successful people act quickly and firmly. They reverse themselves rarely, and only when new facts arise. Decisiveness is also a key element in good luck. Opportunity does not linger. When presented with a good chance—act on it. "Time dissipates energy," an agent once told me. Slowness does not protect you. It dampens or negates opportunities.

Quick and decisive action should not be confused with impulsiveness. If you are following the other rules laid out here, you will not act on blind impulse. Rather, you will have sufficient information about yourself and your surroundings, and sufficient preparation, so that you will be able to move dexterously when the Wheel of Fortune stops where you are standing. Intuition arises not from impulse but from amassing and storing huge amounts of relevant information on which you can immediately draw. When opportunity arrives, the prepared person has "data banks" on which to rely.

Fortune strikes with speed. I know a brilliant singer-songwriter who had top-ten hits in the 1990s.

She said that when fame came her way "it all happened so quickly." As a skilled performer and artist, she was ready. Not everything went smoothly, of course. But she sailed to the top of the charts with her vision and her integrity intact. She continues to produce important work today.

When people are searching for a job or some kind of breakthrough, I always remind them that no matter how many opportunities seem to slip through their fingers "it takes only one yes." Be on the lookout for that "one yes." And be ready to seize it. It doesn't matter what transpired before, or how many heartaches preceded it. They will be forgotten once the "yes" arrives.

A philosopher once asked me: "What do you do when someone offers you a gift?" I looked back at him blankly. "You accept it!" he said. This is exactly what life is like: When something good comes your way—a financial offer, a job, an opportunity, a healthy relationship—do not dither or go into a Hamlet routine. If it's the wrong opportunity you can just as adroitly handle it with a quick no. The unluckiest thing you can do is to demonstrate half-heartedness, delay, or silence. No employer or backer worth having will respect that. He or she wants to know that your dedication or decisiveness matches his own. When chances reach you, act on them.

None of these practices will abrogate every snafu or bad turn. But the 10 Rules of Good Luck ensure your ability to maximize every opportunity that reaches you—and that a greater number of opportunities will reach you.

Action Step
Your Good-Luck Checklist

One of the most intriguing and little-known books of self-help literature offers a straightforward and ethical recipe for cultivating good fortune. The book is *How to Attract Good Luck* by economist, journalist, and diplomat A.H.Z. Carr. Although the 1952 book sounds like a gambling guide, it is anything but. The author served as an economic advisor in the presidential administrations of Franklin Roosevelt and Harry Truman, and spent time on economic and diplomatic missions in Europe and the Far East. Carr amassed a great deal of experience observing how most personal misfortune arises from impetuous or shortsighted behavior.

By luck, Carr was referring not to blind chance but rather to how we can bend circumstances to our favor through healthful patterns of behavior. Here I digest some of Carr's insights. Notice how good ethics are at the core of many of them:

- Demonstrate "unexpected friendliness" to colleagues, strangers, or casual acquaintances. In the history of religion and myth, displays of unwarranted hospitality or friendliness often prove the turning point that results in rewards being showered on someone who unknowingly aids an angel, the gods, or a disguised royal.

- Pursue topics or lines of work for which you feel zest. This is a recipe for fortuitous connections and relationships.

- Boredom is a harbinger of bad luck. Boredom leads you to rash or frivolous actions in pursuit of relief and excitement. Stay busy and engaged.

- Generosity is almost always rewarded one way or another.

- Watch for "small chances" to accomplish your aims. A small step, either in conjunction with other small steps or by itself, can produce unexpected results.

- Stay alert for larger "critical chances"—be watchful.

- "It is lucky to know what we want," Carr writes. Focus brings you right action.

- Never imagine yourself more formidable or skilled than you really are. Be realistic about your current level of abilities and where they must grow.

- Healthful self-respect keeps you out of trouble.

- Avoid hyper-competitive colleagues and acquaintances. "Those who make us feel competitive," Carr writes, "easily can tempt us into unlucky displays of egotism."

- Always look for ways to turn chance events into good use.

- William James: "A single successful effort of moral volition, such as saying 'no' to some habitual temptation, or performing some courageous act, will launch a man on a higher level of energy for days or weeks, will give him a new range of power."

- Prejudice brings bad luck.

- Ethical courage, not impulsiveness, cloyingness, or truculence, imbues you with nobility.

- Defending a loved one is almost always a lucky act.

- Acting without integrity invites misfortune.

- Envy moves you toward foolish actions and pettiness.

- Carr: "Any effort we make, however slight, to prevent the dictation of our behavior by insecurity feelings is a step toward luckiness."

11

The 10-Day Miracle Challenge

Napoleon Hill believed strongly in writing down goals. He consistently emphasized the need to commit your aims to paper—a practice that I urge people to stick to rather than using a tablet or device. The very act of committing something to paper represents an inceptive, tactile projection of your intention in the world. It is actual. And you will feel this.

In that vein, I want to offer you a powerful exercise that can help you attain a near-term goal, especially one that is urgently felt and highly specific. Like paying your rent. Landing a job. Or meeting a mate. At first glance it can seem gimmicky. But look again. And then try it.

First, let me offer some background that brought me to this exercise. A friend of mine studied physics in the graduate program at Columbia University. As it happened, he placed a lot of stock in unconventional

ideas—including methods like astrology that would
have elicited smirks from many (though not all) of his
department colleagues. In fact, he had a particular talent—and respect for—daily horoscopes. The same
sun-sign columns that run online and in newspapers.
I collegially questioned the method. "It's a trick," he
replied. "But sometimes a trick works."

Indeed, the sole question that really matters in
all mystical or therapeutic methods is: does it work? I
have found that often a therapeutic, spiritual, or goal-
based exercise works or fails based on whether the
wished-for outcome can reach you along "established
lines." That means you must pay attention to practical
and sometimes already-established channels of arrival
and fulfillment. Working with established lines is one
of the subtlest and most important points in practical
spirituality. Wallace D. Wattles put it this way in his
1910 *The Science of Getting Rich:*

> In creating, the Formless seems to move
> according to the lines of motion it has estab-
> lished; the thought of an oak tree does not
> cause the instant formation of a full-grown
> tree, but does start in motion the forces which
> will produce the tree, along established lines of
> growth. Every thought of form, held in think-
> ing Substance, causes the creation of the form,
> but always, or at least generally, along lines of
> growth and action already established. The
> thought of a house of a certain construction,
> if it were impressed upon Formless Substance,
> might not cause the instant formation of the

house; but it would cause the turning of creative energies already working in trade and commerce into such channels as to result in the speedy building of the house. And if there were no existing channels through which the creative energy could work, then the house would be formed directly from primal substance without waiting for the slow processes of the organic and inorganic world.

This means that your goal is likely to reach you along familiar or preexisting channels. For example, if you seek the cure of an illness, the likelihood is not that your illness will anomalously lift, but rather that you will discover a network of treatments that produce recovery. If you are looking for employment, the odds are that you will make connections and find leads that will deliver you to what you need—far less likely is that someone will simply present you an offer. I believe that through myriad channels, including the agencies of the mind, we can heighten and hasten the arrival of answers through established channels.

Some practitioners of chaos magick and other ceremonial practices insist that, in order for metaphysical methods to work, by whatever means, there must be a clear avenue of arrival. For example, if you wish for love but dwell as a loner there is little obvious channel of delivery. But if you wish for love and actively circulate among people, you are providing an established means for your fulfillment. This exercise is not about just "showing up;" rather it is about selecting an aim that has a viable means of arrival, which permits the expressiveness of possibilities. An aim that is less direct may also come to fruition, but, depending on what you bring to it, it will require a longer and more complex interval.

Each person must study and consider this step for him or herself. Are you asking for something that fits the context of your life, practices, and habits? Is there a foreseeable method of delivery? On a related note, are you neglecting or overlooking *patterns of delivery*? You must steadily watch for what you want, especially since it may reach you in unfamiliar ways. Your need may be fulfilled in a manner that you do not acknowledge unless you are watching carefully.

With these ground rules in mind, we'll now move into what I call the 10-Day Miracle Challenge. It is very simple but, as the title implies, very powerful. It works according to these six steps:

1. Decide on something that you truly and passionately want in your life, and which represents an authentic (even if rarified) possibility within the fabric of our physical order.

2. Write it down—your wish should be easily boiled down to a single-sentence, such as "I have a peaceful new home nearby."

3. Set a fixed period of time—in this case 10 days—by which to receive your aim.

4. Draw up a grid of 10 boxes and consecutively cross one out each day to countdown toward your aim.

5. Every day, as often as you can and as much as you can, pray, visualize, affirm, and meditate upon the realization of your wish. Think of it constantly.

6. Finally—and here is the most important part— watch carefully for the arrival of your aim, *and take care not to overlook or discount the means by which it arrives.*

Your wish could reach you in a viable but surprising manner, fulfilling your need but arriving in a different fashion from anything you expected. Or your wish could arrive along such seemingly mundane or ordinary lines that you are apt to miss it, and hence overlook the realization of the thing desired.

The point of this exercise is that our needs are often fulfilled, at least in potential, through channels that we are prone to neglect because the arrival doesn't fit our preconceptions, or the arrival happens in such a seemingly mundane fashion that we discount it. You may, for example, wish for recovery from a muscle injury, but at the same time reject an invitation to a yoga or energy-medicine class, or the sanctioned advice of a teacher, therapist, or physician. Again: life-events generally reach us through previously established lines. Hence, the thing desired may arrive in ways that *seem* ordinary even though they are your royal road to fulfillment.

I want to share a joke that drives home this point. During a flood a minister fled to the roof of his church to avoid being swept away in the waters. A man in a raft came by and told him to come aboard. The minister refused. "God will save me," he said. Someone rowed by in a boat and urged him to come on it. But again the minister refused. "God will save me," he said. Finally, a helicopter appeared overhead and dropped a ladder. But the man waved it away. "God will save me!" he yelled. The floodwaters overtook the minister and he drowned. Upon reaching heaven he protested to God, "I've served you all my life! Why didn't you save me?" To which God replied: "I didn't save you? I sent the raft, I sent the boat, I sent the helicopter..."

The lesson is: Remain open. Take the road when it appears. Reject nothing out of hand. And never neglect established means. Watch for them.

Action Step
Your Next Aim

The 10-Day Miracle Challenge deals with near-term goals. It does not supplant or substitute for your Definite Chief Aim—a goal toward which you orient your entire life. Your Definite Chief Aim is something toward which you feel impassioned, wholly dedicated, and ethically certain. Events may come and go; but a Definite Chief Aim serves as a guiding beacon for all that you do.

Someone recently asked me whether a Definite Chief Aim can change. And under what circumstances.

Since life is dynamic, your Definite Chief Aim may change over the years. But when altering your aim, you must ensure that you are not just blowing with the winds. A true goal, like a home, should sustain you for many years. A goal should not be for the relief of occasional discomfort or frustration, but rather should express something fundamental within you.

When considering—or revising—your goal, spend a great deal of time in prayer or meditation. Carefully write down lists of what you truly want from life. Be exquisitely honest—and private. You may wish to confide in a trusted friend, guide, or co-seeker—but do so only if you feel that person can really help you. Avoid idle talk.

For many years, my Definite Chief Aim has been based in my work as a historian of alternative spirituality. That aim has brought me wonderful things, and fulfilled some of my deepest yearnings.

But, as I ponder life from the vantage point of this writing, I feel that my aim may be shifting. I feel driven to fulfill some my earliest childhood yearnings, but not to repeat old thought or emotional patterns. I sense a shift developing within me toward a new aim.

The birth of a new aim sometimes requires revisiting your most nascent memories. Most of us have a special dream from childhood, a literal nighttime dream, which we recall with vividness. When I was about four years old, I dreamed that Eleanor, a deaf girl in our Queens, NY, neighborhood, was kidnapped or taken away by some shadowy adult figures.

I convened an ad-hoc rescue party among neighborhood kids. Standing in a circle, I told my friends: "We gotta rescue Eleanor," Something in that dream holds the key to my next aim.

What is yours?

12

Self-Help for the Secular

In the previous chapter I described the 10-Day Miracle Challenge, which may smack too much of crystals and magic for some readers. (I still urge you to try it and draw your conclusions after the fact.) For those readers who love Napoleon Hill but have few uses for concepts like Infinite Mind, the extra-physical capacities of intuition, or mental causation, I want to offer two powerful—and decidedly materialist—approaches to maximizing your inner abilities and outpicturing your aims. The first is called "Psycho-Cybernetics" and the second is "conscious autosuggestion."

The program of self-development and reconditioning known as Psycho-Cybernetics was devised by a pioneering reconstructive surgeon, Maxwell Maltz, in 1960, and won the allegiance of a wide-range of professional athletes, as well as cultural figures including surrealist artist Salvador Dalí (who struck up a close friendship with Maltz), actress Jane Fonda, and First Lady Nancy Reagan.

In short, Maltz believed that self-image is destiny—and self-image *can be changed.*

His epiphanic moment arrived this way: As a cosmetic surgeon, Maltz was among the first generation to perfect reconstructive surgical techniques. Educated at Columbia, Maltz began treating patients in the 1920s; they included victims of burns and accidents, and others who suffered deformities or birth defects (real and exaggerated), which impaired their daily functioning. After years of medical practice, Maltz made a startling observation: Most of his patients did experience a marked improvement in self-image following successful surgeries—yet a small but persistent number did not, and the clinician wondered at this. Why, he asked, was the low self-image of some patients apparently resistant to an improvement in appearance? And what is this thing that we call "self-image?" Where is it from?

Maltz grew convinced that self-image is, to a large extent, the result of self-perceptions and unconscious messages that you internalize and constantly, often unknowingly, repeat to yourself starting from your earliest age. Such a pattern can be crippling or uplifting—*and it can be altered.*

This insight formed the basis of Maltz's 1960 bestseller, *Psycho-Cybernetics*, a book that retains a loyal readership today. In *Psycho-Cybernetics*, Maltz argued that your mind functions according to the self-regulating system of cybernetics, a term popularized in 1948 by mathematician Norbert Weiner. Cybernetics describes the mechanism behind a heat-seeking missile, which, once programmed, carries out its directive with flawless self-correction. In a similar sense, you too function, Maltz wrote, as a sophisticated, circuit-loop mechanism—yet unlike engineered apparatuses, or even computers, you operate on self-suggestion.

Maltz's program for reconditioning is not for the weak-willed. It is rigorous. In brief, it requires:

1. At least a half-hour a day of deep-relaxation meditation.

2. Another half-hour of self-guided visualization-based meditation, in which you picture yourself and your life exactly as you want it to be, within the categories of reason. (As with the 10-Day Miracle Challenge, canniness and emotional functionality are prerequisites.)

3. A steady, supplemental practice of affirmations, visualizing, and journaling.

Lest this sound too easy, consider: Everything in our lives—especially in the age of hand-held devices unknown in Maltz's time—conspires to rob us of periods of meditation, meaningful self-reflection (versus morbid self-interest), and inner quiet. Have you ever tried to meditate for two thirty-minute periods a day? It's more difficult than it sounds, especially if you already have a regular meditative practice to which the Psycho-Cybernetics exercises are added or accommodated.

So, to return to our question in the previous chapter: *does it work?* My personal experience is: yes—but with two important caveats:

1) The program requires a great deal of self-discipline and inner effort. If there is a secret key to every self-help program, it is absolute, ravenous hunger for self-change. Absent that, self-help is a hobby. With the right degree of hunger, any legitimate program—from the twelve-steps to talk therapy—can make a difference. But never underestimate the depth of passion that must be present to sustain and drive your efforts. As CS Lewis put it: "All depends on really wanting."

2) Maltz died in 1975, before the neurologic and biologic antecedents of our psychology were well understood. I think he underestimated the influence and mysteries of temperamental and characterological traits. For example, every sensitive parent notices that his or her children enter the world—from the earliest days of infancy—with pronounced personality markings, which follow them all their lives. My two sons, ages 12 and 15 as of this writing, displayed temperamental traits from literally the moment they emerged from the womb. I recognize these characteristics in them today. The nature-versus-nurture debate is like a circle with no clear demarcation where one influence ends and another begins. I believe that Maltz, partly due to his generation, overestimated conditioning and underestimated the impact of intrinsic personality, and how biochemistry tends one person toward exuberance and another toward depression.

*   *   *

Even with these caveats, all but the most sectarian determinists would agree that conditioning is a seismic force. Indeed, the very fact of intrinsic personality traits makes conditioning all the more consequential insofar as your conditioned self informs how you navigate intrinsic aspects of character and temperament.

Maltz's insights effectively set the template for all secular forms of popular self-help and motivational philosophy. If you attend a business-oriented or life-coaching self-help program—one with a non-spiritual tone—chances are you are imbibing material from Maltz.

I have a special love for Maltz's program because it conveys a sense of epic hope about the potential of the individual to redirect his life, without requiring any belief system at the door. Psycho-Cybernetics envisions the individual as capable of conquering greater heights than programs that just seem to rearrange the lawn furniture of the mind.

The program's only requirement is zeal to experiment. Different people will, of course, have different results from, and responses to, Maltz's approach. But consider: What more noble undertaking is there than to strive to improve your nature, and strengthen your sense of self-direction? All of it attempted without a sectarian bent, or a necessary leap of religious faith.

Another of my heroes is the early twentieth-century French mind theorist Emile Coué (1857–1926), the pioneer of conscious autosuggestion. Coué is one of the most significant figures in modern motivational philosophy; yet mention of his name will evince blank looks from most people today. Coué, who earned both adulation and jeers during his lifetime, devised a simple, mantra-based method of self-reprograming, which has recently been validated across a wide range of disciplines, often by researchers who are unaware of the inceptive insights upon which their studies rest. I believe that Coué's methods not only deserve new credit and respect, but also hold promise for contemporary seekers and anyone looking for self-directed methods of therapy.

Coué proposed a formula of using mantras or affirmations to reprogram your psyche along the lines of confidence, enthusiasm, and wellness. His methods prefigured the work of figures like Maltz, Napoleon Hill, Neville Goddard, and Anthony Robbins, as well as recent clinical developments in sleep, neuro, placebo, and psychical research. Indeed, at one time many thousands of people in America and Europe swore by Coué's approach. His key mantra—"Day by day, in every way, I am getting better and better"—was repeated by The Beatles and a wide range of therapists and spiritual writers. In rediscovering Coué, you will be able to determine for yourself if his simple approach works. It requires only seconds each day.

Before exploring Coué's method and its application, it is useful to understand his unusual background, which also helps illuminate the birth of motivational philosophy.

Born in Brittany in 1857, Emile Coué developed an early interest in hypnotism, which he pursued through a mail-order course from Rochester, New York. Coué more rigorously studied hypnotic methods in the late

1880s with physician Ambroise-Auguste Liébeault. The French therapist Liébeault was one of the founders of the so-called Nancy School of hypnotism, which promoted hypnotism's therapeutic uses. Leaving behind concepts of occultism and cosmic laws, many of the Nancy hypnotists saw their treatment as a practical form of suggestion, mental reprograming, and psychotherapy.

This was Coué's view, bolstered by personal experience. While working as a pharmacist at Troyes in northwestern France in the early 1900s, Coué made a startling discovery. Patients responded better to medications when he spoke in praise of the formula. Coué came to believe that the imagination aided not only in recovery but also one's general sense of wellbeing. From this insight, Coué developed his method of conscious autosuggestion. It was a form of waking hypnosis that involved repeating confidence-building mantras in a relaxed or semiconscious state.

Coué argued that many of us suffer from poor self-image. This gets unconsciously reinforced because your *willpower*, or drive to achieve, is overcome by your *imagination*, by which he meant one's habitual self-perceptions. "When the will and the imagination are opposed to each other," Coué wrote in 1922, "it is always the *imagination* which *wins*..." By way of example, he asked people to think of walking across a wooden plank laid on the floor—obviously an easy task. But if the same plank is elevated high off the ground, the task becomes fraught with fear even though the physical demand remains the same. This, Coué asserted, is what we are constantly doing on a mental level when we *imagine* ourselves as worthless or weak.

These insights drove the autosuggestive pioneer toward his signature achievement. Coué believed that through the power of self-suggestion or autosuggestion any individual, with nearly any problem, could self-induce the same kinds of positive results he observed in Troyes. In pursuit of an overarching method, Coué devised his self-affirming mantra: "Day by day, in every way, I am getting better and better." The mind theorist made the phrase famous through lecture tours of Europe and the U.S. in the early 1920s. Although few people today have heard of Coué many still recognize his formula.

To critics, however, Coué reflected everything that was fickle and unsound about modern mind metaphysics and motivational philosophies. How, they wondered, could anyone believe that this singsong little mantra—"Day by day, in every way, I am getting better and better"—could solve *anything*? But in a facet of Coué's career that is often overlooked, he demonstrated considerable insight, later validated by sleep researchers and others, in how he prescribed *using* the formula.

Coué said that you must recite the "day by day" mantra just as you're drifting off to sleep at night, when you're hovering within that very relaxed state between wakefulness and sleep. Sleep researchers now call these moments hypnagogia. It is an intriguing state of mind during which you possess sensory awareness, but your perceptions of reality bend and morph, like images from a Salvador Dalí painting. During hypnagogia, your mind is extremely supple and suggestible. Coué understood this by observation and deemed it the period to gently whisper to yourself twenty times: "Day by day, in every way, I am getting better and better." He didn't want you to rouse yourself from your near-sleep state by counting, so he recommended knotting a small string twenty times and then using this device like rosary beads to mark off your repetitions. He also said to repeat the same procedure at the very moment when you wake in the morning, which is sometimes called hypnopompia. It is similar to the nighttime state insofar as you occupy a consciousness shadow world yet possess sufficient cognition to direct your mental workings.

Coué insisted that his mantra-based routine would reprogram your mind and uplift your abilities. Was he correct? There's one way to find out, at least for your own private purposes: try it. We must never place ourselves above "simple" ideas. I have been influenced by the spiritual teacher Jiddu Krishnamurti (1895–1986). He emerged from the Vedic tradition but was an unclassifiable voice. Krishnamurti observed that the greatest impediment to self-development and independent thought is the wish for respectability. Nothing does more to stunt personal experiment, the teacher said, than the certainty that you must follow the compass point of accepted inquiry. Once you grow fixated on that compass point, nearly everything that you read, hear, and encounter gets evaluated on whether it moves you closer to or further from its perceived direction. This makes independent experiment extremely difficult. But if you're unafraid of a little hands-on philosophy, Coué presents the perfect opportunity. He intended his mantra to serve all purposes and circumstances. But you can also craft your own simple mantra that reflects a specific desire. However, you might want to start with Coué's original to get comfortable with the practice.

If you need further inducement to self-experiment, it may help you to realize that Coué's influence travelled in remarkable directions. The Beatles tried Coué's method and apparently liked it. References to Coué appear in some of their songs. In 1967, Paul McCartney used Coué's mantra in the infectious chorus of *Getting Better*: "It's getting better all the time . . ." and the lyrics paid further tribute to the healer: "You gave me the word, I finally heard / I'm doing the best that I can." John Lennon recited Coué's formula in his 1980 song *Beautiful Boy*: "Before you go to sleep, say a little prayer: Every day, in every way, it's getting better and better."

Beyond the Fab Four, placebo researchers at Harvard Medical School recently validated one of Coué's core insights. In January 2014, clinicians from Harvard's program in placebo studies published a paper reporting that migraine sufferers responded better to medication when given "positive information" about a drug. This was the same observation Coué had made in the early 1900s. Harvard's study was considered a landmark because it suggested that the placebo response is operative all the time. It was the first study to use suggestion, in this case news about a drug's efficacy, in connection with an active drug rather than an inert substance, and, hence, found that personal expectation impacts how, and to what extent, we experience an active drug's benefits. Although the Harvard paper echoed Coué's original insight, it made no mention of him.*

I wondered whether the researchers had Coué in mind when they designed the study. I asked one of the principals, who did not respond. So, I contacted the director of Harvard Medical School's program in placebo studies, Ted Kaptchuk, a remarkable and inquisitive clinician who also worked on the study. "Of course I know about Coué," Kaptchuk told me. "'I'm getting better day by day . . .'" He agreed that the migraine study coalesced with Coué's observations, though the researchers were not thinking of him when they designed it.

Coué's impact appears under the radar in an unusual range of places. An influential twentieth-century British Methodist minister named Leslie D. Weatherhead looked for a way that patients and seekers could effectively convince themselves of the truth and power of their affirmations, especially when such statements chaffed against circumstantial reality, such as in cases of addiction or persistently low self-worth. Weatherhead was active in the Oxford Group in the 1930s, which preceded Alcoholics Anonymous in pursuit of religious-therapeutic methods. In using suggestions or affirmations to improve one's sense of self-worth and puncture limiting beliefs, the minister was attempting to update Coué.

---

* "Altered Placebo and Drug Labeling Changes the Outcome of Episodic Migraine Attacks" by Slavenka Kam-Hansen, et al, *Science Translational Medicine*, 08 Jan 2014: Vol. 6, Issue 218, pp. 218ra5.

Weatherhead understood that affirmations—such as "I am confident and poised"—could not penetrate the "critical apparatus" of the human mind, which he compared to "a policeman on traffic duty." Other physicians and therapists similarly noted the problem of affirmations lacking emotional persuasiveness. Some therapists insisted that affirmations had to be credible to get through to the subject; no reasonable person would accept exaggerated self-claims, a point that Coué had also made. While Weatherhead agreed with these critiques, he believed that the rational "traffic cop" could be eluded by two practices. The first was the act of repetition: "A policeman on duty who refuses, say, a cyclist, the first time, might ultimately let him into the town if he presented himself again and again," he wrote in 1951. Continuing the metaphor, Weatherhead took matters further:

> I can imagine that a cyclist approaching a town might more easily elude the vigilance of a policeman if the attempt to do so were made in the half-light of early dawn or the dusk of evening. Here also the parable illumines a truth. The early morning, when we waken, and the evening, just as we drop off to sleep, are the best times for suggestions to be made to the mind.

As Weatherhead saw it, the hypnagogic state—again, the drowsy state between wakefulness and sleep, generally experienced when a person is drifting off in the evening or coming to in the morning—is a period of unique psychological flexibility, when ordinary barriers are down. This is pure Couéism. Moreover, this fact probably reflects why people suffering from depression or anxiety report the early waking hours as the most difficult time of day—the rational defenses are slackened. If the individual could use the gentlest effort to repeat affirmations, without rousing himself fully to a waking state, the new ideas could penetrate, Coué and Weatherhead believed.

Mystic and teacher Neville Goddard (1905–1972) made a similar point about the malleability of the hypnagogic mind. So did the twentieth-century psychical researcher and scientist Charles Honorton (1946–1992), who used this observation as a basis for testing the potential for telepathy between individuals. Honorton believed that a hypnagogic state was, in effect, "prime time" for the reception of extrasensory communication.

In the early 1970s, Honorton and his collaborators embarked on a long-running series of highly regarded psi experiments, known as the *ganzfeld* experiments (German for "whole field"). These trials were designed to induce a hypnagogic state in a "receiver." The subject was placed, seated or reclining, in a soft-lit or darkened room and fitted with eye covers and earphones to create a state of comfortable sensory deprivation. Seated in another room, a "sender" would attempt to telepathically convey an image to the receiver. After the sending period ended, the receiver was asked to select the correct image among four—three images were decoys, establishing a chance hit-rate of 25 percent. Experimenters found that receivers consistently made higher-than-chance selections of the correct "sent" image. Honorton collaborated with avowed skeptic and research psychologist Ray Hyman in reviewing the data from a wide range of ganzfeld experiments. The psychical researcher and the skeptic jointly wrote: "We agree that there is an overall significant effect in this data base that cannot be reasonably explained by selective reporting or multiple analysis."* Honorton added, "Moreover, we agree that the significant outcomes have been produced by a number of different investigators."

Hyman insisted that none of this was proof of psi, though he later acknowledged that "contemporary ganzfeld experiments display methodological and statistical sophistication well above previous parapsychological research. Despite better controls and careful use of statistical inference, the investigators seem to be getting significant results that do not appear to derive from the more obvious flaws of previous research." Although serious psychical research has come under withering, and often unfair, criticism in recent years, the ganzfeld experiments have remained relatively untouched—and their methodological basis comes from the insights of Coué.

Coué's presence emerges, too, in popular literature. One of the most enduring and beguiling pieces of popular metaphysics on the American scene is a 28-page pamphlet called *It Works* written in 1926 by a Chicago ad executive named Roy Herbert Jarrett. I noted Jarrett's efforts earlier in the chapter, "Mind Power and 'the Zone'." To recap, his method is to write down and focus on your desires—first, you must clarify your need; second, write it down and think of it always; and third, tell no one what you are doing to maintain mental steadi-

---

* "A Joint Communiqué: The Psi Ganzfeld Controversy" by Ray Hyman and Charles Honorton, *Journal of Parapsychology*, vol. 50, December 1986.

ness. Plain enough, perhaps, but the seeker's insights rested on the deeper aspects of Couéism.

In the early 1920s, Jarrett and many other Americans thrilled to news of Coué's mantra. The "Miracle Man of France" briefly grew into an international sensation as American newspapers featured *Ripley's-Believe-It-Or-Not*-styled drawings of Coué, looking like a goateed magician and gently displaying his knotted string at eye level like a hypnotic device. In early 1923, Coué made a three-week lecture tour of America, making one of his final stops in Jarrett's hometown of Chicago, where the Frenchman spoke at Orchestra Hall.

In a raucous scene, a crowd of more than two thousand demanded that the therapist help a paralytic man who had been seated onstage. Coué defiantly told the audience that his autosuggestive treatments could work only on illnesses that originated in the mind. "I have not the magic hand," he insisted. Nonetheless, Coué approached the man and told him to concentrate on his legs and to repeat, "It is passing, it is passing." The seated man struggled up and haltingly walked. The crowd exploded. Coué rejected any notion that his "cure" was miraculous and insisted that the man's disease must have been psychosomatic.

To some Americans, Coué's message of self-affirmation held special relevance for oppressed people. The pages of Marcus Garvey's newspaper, *Negro World*, echoed Coué's day-by-day mantra in an editorial headline: "Every Day in Every Way We See Drawing Nearer and Nearer the Coming of the Dawn for Black Men." The paper editorialized that Marcus Garvey's teachings provided the same "uplifting psychic influence" as Coué's.

Coué took a special liking to Americans. He found American attitudes a refreshing departure from what he knew back home. "The French mind," he wrote in 1923, "prefers first to discuss and argue on the fundamentals of a principle before inquiring into its practical adaptability to every-day life. The American mind, on the contrary, immediately sees the possibilities of it, and seeks ... to carry the idea further even than the author of it may have conceived."

The therapist could have been describing salesman-seeker Roy Herbert Jarrett and many others in the American positive-mind tradition. "A short while ago," Jarrett wrote in 1926, the year of Coué's death, "Dr. Emile Coué came to this country and showed thousands of people how to help themselves. Thousands of others spoofed at the idea, refused his assistance and are today where they were before his visit."

Just as Coué had observed about American audiences, Jarrett boldly expanded on the uses of autosuggestion. Sounding the keynote of the American metaphysical tradition, Jarrett believed that subconscious-mind training did more than just recondition the mind: it activated a divine inner power that served to out-picture a person's mental images into the surrounding world. "I call this power 'Emmanuel' (God in us)," Jarrett wrote. In essence, the entirety of American positive-mind metaphysics rests on Coué-style methods.

Coué's instincts spoke to the individual's profoundest wish for self-help and personal empowerment. It is my observation, as both a historian and seeker, that some people across generations have experienced genuine help through his ideas. So, once more, I invite you to disregard expectation and to experiment with Coué's method. We all possess the private agency of self-experiment; indeed, it may be the area in life in which we are most free. Yet we often get so wrapped up in the possibilities of digital culture and the excitement of social media that we neglect the technology of thought, through which we may be able to significantly reform some aspect of ourselves and our surrounding world.

It may be that the ideas of this mind pioneer, a figure so under-recognized in today's culture, offer the very simplicity and effectiveness that you are seeking.

Action Step
How to Practice
Conscious Autosuggestion

For a brief but complete explanation of how to use the day-by-day mantra I am providing the words of Emile Coué himself from his 1922 book, *Self-Mastery Through Conscious Autosuggestion:*

> Every morning on awakening and every evening as soon as you are in bed, close your eyes, and without fixing your attention in what you say, pronounce twenty times, just loud enough so that you may hear your own words, the following phrase, using a string with twenty knots in it for counting:

"DAY BY DAY, IN EVERY WAY, I AM GETTING BETTER AND BETTER."

The words: "IN EVERY WAY" being good for anything and everything, it is not necessary to formulate particular autosuggestions.

Make this autosuggestion with faith and confidence, and with the certainty that you are going to obtain what you desire.

Moreover, if during the day or night, you have a physical or mental pain or depression, immediately affirm to yourself that you are not going to CONSCIOUSLY contribute anything to maintain the pain or depression, but that it will disappear quickly. Then isolate yourself as much as possible, close your eyes, and pass your hand across your forehead, if your trouble is mental, or over the aching part of your body if physical, and repeat quickly, moving your lips, the words: "IT PASSES, IT PASSES," etc. Continue this as long as may be necessary, until the mental or physical pain has disappeared, which it usually does within twenty or twenty-five seconds. Begin again every time you find it necessary to do so.

Like the first autosuggestion given above, you must repeat this one also with absolute faith and confidence, but calmly, without effort. Repeat the formula as litanies are repeated in church.

13

The Esoteric Golden Rule

At certain points in my personal search I have felt
frozen—as if some unnamed factor was stymying my
progress. I have sometimes felt periodically limited in
my ability to envision and pursue higher possibilities for
myself and others. I get stuck in a holding pattern.

I learned from Napoleon Hill that the way out is
often found through the so-called Golden Rule. The
precept "do unto others as you would have them do unto
you" runs through virtually every religious and ethical
teaching, from the Talmud to the Vedas to the Bhagavad
Gita. Dubbed the Golden Rule in late-seventeenth century England, this dictum can seem overly familiar or
clichéd. But the Golden Rule holds an inner truth that
can make all the difference in your life.

In *The Law of Success*, Hill related the Golden
Rule to the phenomenon of autosuggestion, or the

suggestions we continually make to ourselves. This is the material we just explored in the section on Emile Coué. The French mind theorist taught that what we internally repeat and believe takes root in our subconscious and shapes our self-image and perceptions of the surrounding world. This is a profound and determinative fact.

But this note carefully: the same autosuggestive process is also triggered by *what we think about others*. "Your thoughts of others are registered in your subconscious mind through the principle of autosuggestion," Hill wrote, "thereby building your own character in exact duplicate." Hence: "You must 'think of others as you wish them to think of you."

Let's consider Hill's point of view more fully:

Stated in another way, every act and every thought you release modifies your own character in exact conformity with the nature of the act or thought, and your character is a sort of center of magnetic attraction, which attracts to you the people and conditions that harmonize with it. You cannot indulge in an act toward another person without having first created the nature of that act in your own thought, and you cannot release a thought without planting the sum and substance and nature of it in your own subconscious mind, there to become a part and parcel of your own character.

Grasp this simple principle and you will understand why you cannot afford to hate or envy another person. You will also understand why you cannot afford to strike back, in kind, at those who do you an injustice. Likewise, you will understand the injunction, "Return good for evil."

When we indulge in fantasies of revenge or score settling—which I've done more times than I can count—we not only shackle ourselves to past wrongs, but also to the wrongs that we would do in exchange. Our acts of violence, whether by thought, word, or hand, subtly reenact themselves in our psyches and perceptions. We are lowered to the level of people we resent or even hate when we counter—mentally or otherwise—their type of behavior. An adjunct to the Golden Rule is: *You become what you do not forgive.*

Conversely, thoughts of generosity and forgiveness add a special solidity to our character, Hill notes, "that gives it life and power."

Our thoughts about ourselves and about others can be seen as an invisible engine that molds our character and experience. This is why it is extremely important to abstain from spreading or listening to gossip, rumor, or character assassination. I do not mean ignoring pleas for justice or exposures of abuse—not at all. But rather the chatter of people, social-media accounts, or shows that frivolously score-settle or traffic in running down or humiliating others.

If you find yourself bumping against personal limits, or having difficulty formulating and acting on your plans, reconsider your relationship to the Golden Rule. It summarizes karma or "cosmic reciprocity" within a compact maxim.

Action Step
No Complaining

We often mislead ourselves that we'll feel better about something—whether a perceived slight, a bad friend, slow service in a restaurant—by venting or complaining about it. But this is a false comfort. Giving voice to a complaint is often a spiral: we not only fail to feel better, but one complaint generally gives rise to others in a repeat cycle.

The complaint cycle can occur in conversation but it often occurs—and in a more pernicious and drawn-out manner—through one's inner talking. Try to observe your inner talking for just five minutes. It frequently consists of complaints, internal eye-rolls, and a listing of anxieties. Attempt to catch yourself complaining within—and stop it. You won't always be able to stop it, but if you catch it early enough it sometimes becomes possible.

In such cases, you will interrupt the pattern of negative self-suggestion. Over time, such internal "stops" will alter your outward behavior. You will eventually grow less attached to complaining as a means of conversation. As with gossip, a startling amount of our conversations consist of an exchange of complaints—about the weather, traffic, the length of lines, about who said what to who, and so on. I know people who sit down in a restaurant—places that many in the world never even get to enter—and almost immediately begin to complain about the placement of the table, the intensity of the air conditioning, the service, and so on. I've done it myself. This kind of habit subtly shapes and degrades our view of the world, ourselves, and our satisfaction within it. If you are not careful, such a habit can engulf and characterize your entire life. I've seen it occur. Today, I make an effort, however fitfully, not to complain in front of my children so they don't pick up this habit from me.

You can practice complaint stoppage at any time of day, even when you're alone. Try for just three hours to desist from internal and external complaining. See how you feel—and watch for what happens.

14

How to Rebound from Disappointment

Sometimes our problems are situational. Some difficulties are based in events or circumstances over which we have limited control, such as job loss or the incidental failure of a plan or project. Napoleon Hill repeatedly noted that the path to success is marked with temporary setbacks, episodic failures, and disappointments. It can be difficult to cope during these periods. But there is a productive way.

An actor once wrote to me seeking advice. He explained that he was absolutely determined to break through in his field—but he found himself harboring a great deal of resentment toward casting directors and others whom he felt had unfairly passed him over. From the perspective of effective thought and action, he wondered what to do. Should he "let go" of his hard feelings as a way to manage?

Frankly, I'm unsure whether any of us fully "let go" of anything. I told him that rather than pursue that elusive and perhaps unnatural goal, he might instead use their rejection as a goad to aim higher. I recounted the story of mystic Neville Goddard who described journeying from his island home of Barbados at age seventeen to study drama in New York City in the early 1920s. On the first day of class, a cruel teacher made Neville "the goat" and, alluding to the newcomer's British-Barbadian accent, pointed him out as one "who would never earn a living using his voice."

"But she did not know the kind of man she was dealing with," Neville recalled. He used the humiliation not only to train his voice—which is now among the most memorable and mellifluous in twentieth-century spiritual oration—but he also went on to a career as a writer and spiritual thinker who influenced figures ranging from Carlos Castaneda to New Age authors Wayne Dyer and Rhonda Byrne to major-league pitcher Barry Zito. Today, Neville is posthumously becoming one of the most respected and widely followed figures on the alternative spiritual scene.

Forgiveness is important to manage relations with people close to us. *Forgiveness should never be asked for*; it is something that only the injured party can give. But forgiveness, acceptance, or "letting go," as virtues, can also feel distant and unnatural. Indeed, an equally—or perhaps more—productive form of response is to use the harm suffered as a springboard to higher self-expression.

Ironically, this is what dramatist John Milton (1608-1674) demonstrates in his portrait of the Eternal Rebel in the early books of *Paradise Lost*. These passages reflect not only some of the most enthralling portraits of psychological self-determination in history, but, somewhat surprisingly, also suggest a higher, nobler, and better way to live; a way toward which many of us may feel drawn, or are at least questioning toward, but are too squeamish to acknowledge.

Consider: Milton's anti-hero neither bows his head in humility, crumples into defeat, or sets himself the task of regaining his former Master's favor. Rather, he famously declares from his subterranean throne:

> *Here we may reign secure, and in my choice*
> *To reign is worth ambition though in Hell:*
> *Better to reign in Hell, then serve in Heav'n.*

In summoning and reviving his defeated troops—those angels who joined him battling what is considered an overbearing and conformity-demanding God—Milton's Lucifer encourages extreme self-reliance:

> *The mind is its own place, and in it self*
> *Can make a Heav'n of Hell, a Hell of Heav'n.*

The fallen angels heed him. In a historically underappreciated passage, one states:

> *To whom we hate. Let us not then pursue*
> *By force impossible, by leave obtain'd*
> *Unacceptable, though in Heav'n, our state*
> *Of splendid vassalage, but rather seek*
> *Our own good from our selves, and from our own*
> *Live to our selves, though in this vast recess,*

Free, and to none accountable, preferring
Hard liberty before the easy yoke of servile Pomp.

I am friendly with a widely known political operative who once suffered a public defeat. I was unsure what to tell him, until the words came to me in an email: "Hard liberty before the easy yoke." My arrow seemed to find its mark. He replied: "Dude!!!!!!!!!!!!!!!!!!!!"

One time I was telling another friend, a thoughtful student of the teachings of Christian mystic Edgar Cayce (1877–1945), that I felt my writing career was stalled. This was around the time I wrote about earlier, when I was supplying free or near-free copy for a bevy of middling alternative-spiritual magazines. Rather than mew to me about non-attachment, my friend stated simply: "It sounds like you need to be writing for better magazines." I could have replied: "Dude!!!!!!!!!!!!!!!!!!!!"

I acted on his advice, and in years immediately ahead I had bylines in places including *The New York Times*, *The Washington Post*, *Politico*, and *The Wall Street Journal*. Not places noted as outlets of occult passion.

Whenever you feel thwarted, assailed, or overlooked, the way to the "high road" may pass through what is traditionally considered the "low"—in other words: be defiant, driven, unbowed, and brave. Consider the psychological possibility that it really is better to live solely from your own ethically informed principles than from another's, whether it be a person or an institution.

Action Step
When All Else Fails

A woman once wrote me saying that her efforts toward manifesting a better, fuller life had hit a dead end. She felt lost, and asked for help. When you feel that your search for achievement has stalled or failed, try these steps:

First, if you do not already, you must have a very clear, even single-minded aim. As you know by now, this is my mantra. Your goal must be passionate—and narrow. Are you focused on one thing, or many? The one thing may satisfy many needs, but it must be singular. Otherwise, you risk dispersing your energies.

Second, you must consider what barrier you're facing. Are you reaching for something that contradicts your inner goals and principles? For example, my passion is to chronicle metaphysical experience—and to do so with integrity, intellect, and practicality. I will not compromise on that. When I go after something that violates my ethics, I experience friction.

Third, if you're a believing person, have you attempted—with total and complete passion—to *pray* for what you want? I believe strongly that a person should never candy-coat, disguise, or soft-pedal what he or she wants from life. After all, from whom would you be hiding it? Pray to whatever Higher Power is real to you. I don't share the widely held New Age attitude that prayer must be accompanied by a feeling of having already received, or a sense of calm certainty, etc. There is no wrong way to pray, just as there is no wrong (or single) way to affirm, a topic to which I return. Pray with every fiber of your being: make it a physical, emotional, and mental experience—one of inner totality. The answer you receive may be yes, no, or something else; but if a Higher Power relates to us, then you *are* entitled to an answer. The biblical matriarchs and patriarchs were not timid about prayer. Be bold.

Fourth, *constantly improve*. Be like a martial artist or master musician who never stops training and preparing for the instance when his or her moment arrives, sometimes in the strangest or most unexpected way. Someone once defined artistry as excellence meeting opportunity. Be excellent and ready. Preparation is never wasted.

15

Unlocking the "Mystery of Sex Transmutation"

Napoleon Hill made a fascinating observation about human nature in *Think and Grow Rich*, which I have repeatedly found to be true:

> The world is ruled, and the destiny of civilization is established, by the human emotions. People are influenced in their actions, not by reason so much as by "feelings." The creative faculty of the mind is set into action entirely by emotions, and *not by cold reason*. The most powerful of all human emotions is that of sex. There are other mind stimulants . . . but no one of them, nor all of them combined, can equal the driving power of sex.

Picking up on Hill's insight about sex energy, I want to explore the uses and applications of this familiar yet little-understood force. Sex energy, Hill argued, is the most powerful mind stimulant and—if properly used—free of all negative side effects.

In his 1948 book *Think Your Way to Wealth*, Hill wrote:

> The emotion of sex is nature's own source of inspiration through which she gives both men and women the impelling desire to create, build, lead, and direct. Every great artist, every great musician, and every great dramatist gives expression to the emotion of sex transmuted into human endeavor. It is also true that men of vision, initiative, and enthusiasm who lead and excel in industry and business owe their superiority to transmuted sex emotion.

This is, in a sense, the taboo subject of Hill's program, one that people are often too embarrassed to talk about at business and motivational conferences. In *Think and Grow Rich* he called it "mystery of sex transmutation."

One of my heroes, Earl Nightingale (1921–1989), a great radio broadcaster and pioneering motivational writer, produced and narrated an abridgment of *Think and Grow Rich* in 1960. This being an earlier generation, the publisher was either too embarrassed or timorous to include sex transmutation as a topic, so Earl changed it to "enthusiasm," producing a vague and forgettable chapter. Hill, to his credit, took a great personal risk years earlier and included a highly innovative and insightful chapter on the topic in his signature book.

And yet, nearly a generation later, Earl Nightingale, who I love, was embarrassed out of using that phraseology in his abridgement.

Now, I've met certain people in the alternative spiritual culture who regard *Think and Grow Rich* as an unserious book. They see it as a book for materially minded people or a book that's too adolescent. Some see it as metaphysics with training wheels. Yet some of the same people will reverse themselves and acknowledge: "Hill's chapter on sex transmutation is one of the best things that's ever been written on the topic." Some today who consider themselves chaos magicians or who are into ceremonial magick or psychological alchemy are actually working with sex transmutation. And one of the method's clearest exponents was the familiar-seeming figure of Napoleon Hill, who few seekers today regard as a radical, yet who wrote perhaps the most practical, most applicable, and broadly readable exploration of the topic.

Hill believed that the sexual impulse is the *universal creative urge of life* within all men and women, and that the sexual impulse represents the urge not only to procreate and propagate the species, but to create *all things*. The great painter, the great artist, the great entrepreneur, the great businessperson, the great activist, the great diplomat—anyone who has something he or she wishes to concretize within the world—has, at their backs, this drive of sexual expression. It often comes out only physically, but it's an expression of the overall creative principle of life seeking to actualize itself.

We generally see sex as strictly physical because that's how we've been conditioned. But Hill is pointing to a higher truth gleaned by Vedic masters, Taoists, Kabbalists, practitioners of Tantra, and others who are involved in chaos magick, ceremonial magick, and sex magick, all of which are interrelated. Across vast stretches of time and culture this diffuse lineage of seekers has converged around the insight that the sexual urge is the life-principle seeking expression. Again, this expression can be manifested through physicality, pleasure, and propagation of the species. Without it we wouldn't be here. But Hill taught that the sexual urge is also at the back of everything that you as a generative being strive to create.

In the ancient Greek-Egyptian philosophy called Hermeticism we're told, "As above, so below." In Scripture we're told, "God created man in his own image." In these and other religious principles what we're really hearing, if you take them seriously, is that *our birthright is generativity and productivity*; we are to function as co-creators within our concentric sphere of existence. And the driving force behind this wish to produce, generate, and create is the sexual urge, of which procreation and pleasure are the physical expressions. But the other expressions appear in everything that the individual produces.

Hill gleaned this truth when very few modern people grasped any such idea. Hill possessed this almost wild yet practical instinct for a topic that's deeply esoteric. He wrote about it plainly. He made it into a practical formula. And the formula is this: *You can consciously harness the forces of sex transmutation by channeling the sexual urge into some other form of creativity.* When you feel the sexual urge, rather than acting on it in the usual way, you *redirect your thoughts toward the thing you wish to create*. This adds intellectual, charismatic, and creative power to your efforts. In fact, Hill wrote that we're using this power all the time—this is occurring whenever a salesman is demonstrating enthusiasm or personal magnetism; whenever an artist is exuding passion; whenever a minister is possessed by some kind of inspiration on the pulpit—that's the sexual urge being transmuted by thought into other channels of expression. The art of sexual transmutation involves harnessing the urge consciously, through a redirection of your thoughts.

It is important to note that Hill is by no means prescribing celibacy. He's not saying that the sexual urge should be sublimated; he's very plain that a proper outlet for sexuality is therapeutic, healthy, and necessary. But he does say that you can cultivate an awareness that sexuality is that raw energy behind everything you wish to accomplish; and, you can, at self-selected moments, *redirect the sexual urge towards whatever creative thing you want to out-picture in the world*. This gives you greater energy, intellect, magnetism, and effectiveness. It places a universal force in service to your efforts.

This perspective on sexuality is interesting in light of our own era, in which it is tempting to ask: Why do accomplished people compromise their entire lives to satisfy the sexual urge? Just prior to this writing, I heard someone at a dinner party asking this very question. You see all these powerful men, titans of politics, of media, of culture, and they're brought down by the inappropriate pursuit of sex. People have asked, why?

Why would you sacrifice everything, and sometimes abuse others, to engage in an act of sex? I think it has something to do with what Hill was getting at. Now, of course, there's a great deal of ego and other factors caught up in it, including entitlement, power, and so forth. But some people engage in a grossly misdirected use of this energy; to some, sexual expression feels like life itself, but it's a misconstrued use. Hill specifically warned about this.

On one hand, this wild, frenzied energy can be directed toward consensual pleasure, toward procreation, and toward productive projects—without it not only would the species not get propagated, but bridges wouldn't get built, diseases wouldn't get cured, and beautiful works of art wouldn't get made. But if you permit that sexual urge to express itself only through physicality—or through an abusive physicality, where questions of consent and human respect are compromised—this powerful principle gets corrupted.

As alluded earlier, sex transmutation is the most under-discussed topic in *Think and Grow Rich* because people find it embarrassing. They find it difficult to talk about. But what I'm describing is a faithful representation of what Hill was driving at, which is a very productive principle. Certainly Hill's analysis has helped me identify some of the exuberance or enthusiasm that I feel towards my subject matter as something that is transmuted sexual energy. Hill even made the observation—and this may sound exaggerated—that if you can direct or transmute your sexual energy in the direction of something you wish to accomplish, your psyche is elevated, at least temporarily, to the status of a genius. That language may seem far-flung—but I must say that I have noticed in the lives of certain people this absolute effectiveness that seems almost superhuman.

Take, for example, the same friend who was raising this question of sexuality at the dinner party. While in his twenties he cofounded one of the most profitable and significant consulting companies in the world. It is now a hugely successful firm on a global scale. People have heard of it. I remember a mutual acquaintance once saying that my friend is almost like a figure from another era, like a Benjamin Franklin, who seems so possessed of energies that he seems larger than life. That is an example of unconscious sexual transmutation. If I talked to him about any of this, he'd probably say, "You're out of your mind!" But he's a perfect exemplar.

I must say, in frankness and speaking from personal experience, that I do bring a degree of sexual transmutation to my work and writing. People sometimes marvel at my work output and ask, "How do you do it?" I believe that some of what Hill is describing is at the back of it. I feel strongly that the topic of sex transmutation should not be neglected or downplayed. It's very esoteric, it's very intriguing, and it's also very practical. Hill did not spell it all out in minute detail. You must personally experiment with it. But I've given you a significant starting point. I believe that your experiments will net the discovery that sex transmutation adds remarkable vigor, charisma, and intellectual power to your efforts.

Action Step
Practicing Sex Transmutation

Since I do not want to leave any questions in your mind as to the elementary steps of sex transmutation, I am laying a simple plan that you can use almost immediately.

Now, when you feel sexual desire what do you generally do? Well, you may engage in a physical act to satisfy the urge. Or you may sublimate the urge and defer satisfaction to some other time. Those are the common responses.

But Hill provided another option, which is filled with portent for your success.

He taught that rather than satisfying or sublimating your desire, you can, *through a mental act*, redirect your desire toward the accomplishment of a cherished task.

Make the *mental effort to channel the sexual urge in the direction of another activity*. Simply shift your thoughts from physical sexual gratification to something else: the completion of a piece of writing; the pursuit of a client; the creation of your art; the achievement of a physical or athletic goal—whatever it is, you must act on it with these redirected sexual energies focused on your task or aim.

Does sexual transmutation work? I have found that it does. Again, you must experiment with it yourself; no one else can fully describe the process and results for you.

Keep in mind, as I have alluded, that the point is *not* to create another orthodoxy or "rule" around sex. Sometimes the physical expression must be honored. Sexual activity, for pleasure or procreation, is necessary for mental, emotional, and physical wellness. But in moments that *you alone choose* you can redirect your sexual urge along the lines of a specific task or activity.

Once you have successfully attempted this you may discover new and varying ways of employing sexual energy. For example, you can also use the act of sex transmutation to cultivate a specific mood or personality trait, such as confidence, courage, or enthusiasm. You may want to attempt this in the short-term for help with a job interview or personal project; or you may want to use this practice in the long-term to rework an aspect of your personality.

Sex transmutation is modern alchemy. Accept no limits on what you may find.

16

Napoleon Hill's
Most Neglected Step

Napoleon Hill's book *The Path to Personal Power* focuses on one of the most neglected steps in his program of success—and one that he personally described as critical to the workability of his overall approach: the formation of a Master Mind group.

In *Think and Grow Rich*, Hill defined the Master Mind (another term he always capitalized) as: "Coordination of knowledge and effort, in a spirit of harmony, between two or more people for the attainment of a definite purpose."

Hill also used the term Master Mind on occasion to refer to a group working not toward one common goal but to accomplish the goals of each individual.

In plain terms, this second type of Master Mind group is, quite simply, a support group or fellowship consisting of two or more members (but usually no more than seven to keep things wieldy), which meets at regular intervals of at least once a week to give support and advice to members on their individual goals. Depending on the nature of the group, members may also offer meditation, prayers, and mental visualization for one another's goals in between weekly meetings.

At its heart, this second type of Master Mind group is a coordinated effort to explore and support one another's purposes and needs. Hill believed that when several people regularly meet in a spirit of comity and mutual support—there can be no divisiveness in the Master Mind—it will enhance the creativity, intuition, and mental faculties of each participant. For this reason, you must select the members of your Master Mind group carefully; the key factors are personal chemistry and cooperation. Divisiveness, political arguments (always keep politics at bay), squabbling, and discursive aims will deplete the functioning of the Master Mind.

I once described *Think and Grow Rich* in a single sentence, which could encompass all of Hill's work: "Emotionalized thought directed toward one passionately held aim—aided by organized planning and the Master Mind—is the root of all accomplishment." This gives you an idea of how central the Master Mind concept is in Hill's system.

"Great power," he concluded of the Master Mind, "can be accumulated through no other principle."

As I noted in the first chapter, the genius—and demand—of Hill's work is that none of his steps are superfluous. Yet in today's digitally removed world it is tempting to skip or ignore this advice. Unless you are already a member of a twelve-step or support group, you are probably accustomed to a "go it alone" approach, not wanting to share intimacies or accommodate your already-busy routine to another meeting. Many of us believe that our success is a matter of inner principle and individual effort, and a group meeting seems mawkish or extraneous. I understand those feelings—I struggle with them myself.

But I can promise you, as a writer and historian who has studied Hill's methods for years and owes his success to them, and as someone who has been a dedicated member of a Master Mind group since fall of 2013, this step is as vital today as when Hill prescribed the Master Mind in the first chapter of his first book, *The Law of Success*, in 1928.

Another characteristic of our cyber-age is that friends and collaborators often live and work far distances part. The members of my Master Mind group are dispersed from Southern California to New Hampshire. We structure things this way: all four participants— each possessed of supportive natures, good humor, and spiritual values—meet at a regularly designated time by conference call once a week. We begin by reading a short statement of principles, and each participant then offers a piece of personal good news from the previous week. Each member then takes a turn describing his wants and needs for the week ahead. After a caller has expressed his wants and needs, each group member suggests advice, ideas, encouragement, and may offer prayer or other forms of support during off times. Our call generally lasts thirty-to-forty-five minutes.

It is important to begin the Master Mind meeting on time, to commence it immediately—eschewing small talk and preliminary chatter to respect people's time—and to cap the meeting at an hour or less, preferably no more than 45 minutes. (Though this differs depending on group size.) This kind of discipline helps prevent drifting of attention or resentment when members are pressed by the clock or when someone may have greater free time or simply more tolerance for meetings. All of us have enough meetings in life. Most are worthless. The Master Mind, by contrast, is vital and potent; as such, its work should be precise.

This collaborative alliance, if conducted with purpose and harmony, will, in time, yield extraordinary results. I can honestly say that my Master Mind group has proven one of the most helpful and dynamic aspects in my and each members' life. Our meetings steady me when I am off course, and give me fresh perspective and an added boost to the week. There are also practical benefits, in which economic and business issues are hashed out. And there may be something more at play.

"No two minds," Hill wrote, "ever come together without, thereby, creating a third invisible, intangible force which may be likened to a third mind." This, to him, was the "psychic" phase of the Master Mind, in which the mind may be likened to an energy that is pooled with that of others to intensify intuitions, ideas, and insights. Everyone in a Master Mind group, Hill said, gains heightened insight through the subconscious minds of all the other members. This produces a more vivid imaginative and mental state in which new ideas "flash" into your awareness, he taught.

Whether you are ready to make the leap to this way of thought—I do, and I explore this more fully in the

Napoleon Hill Success Course book *The Power of the Master Mind*—I vow to you that the Master Mind will play an invaluable and practical role in your pursuit of achievement.

Action Step
Finding Your Master Mind Group

One evening at a Denver workshop a participant asked me the following question, which I provide here with my reply. It likely addresses your most immediate or lingering questions about finding a Master Mind group.

Q: *How do I find or form a Master Mind group?*
A: That is the big question everybody has. I was fortunate in that I was invited into my Master Mind group. It was a pre-existing group and some people I knew through my own interests in New Thought invited me into it. I joined a group that was at the time five members, and it's undergone some different permutations, but it's still basically the same core group.

If you don't have a Master Mind group that presents itself for you to join, you have to start your own. You can start your own with as few as two people. It's that simple. You just need to find one other friend or colleague of similar values. Likely, you'd want to find somebody who has either read or who is interested in reading *Think and Grow Rich* and other works by Napoleon Hill, and who has a vested interest in mind metaphysics, in New Thought, in Unity, and programs of mental causation and Psycho-Cybernetics, what have you.

The group can be spiritually oriented or it can be less so, maybe leaning more in a secular, business-motivational direction. Either one is fine. The only critical ingredient is group harmony. If your group is more spiritually oriented, and you are comfortable with concepts of prayer and mental visualization and affirmations, so long as everybody's on board with that and comfortable with that and there's nobody sitting on the bench while such things are being talked about, then you're good to go.

Again, the beautiful thing is, and I must emphasize this, it can be as few as two people. I wouldn't go larger than seven people because that can start to get a little bit unwieldy, which was something that Napoleon Hill made note of. But, if you've got one other friend or colleague or collaborator of like-minded principles, you have a Master Mind group.

The key thing of course, too, is that you need a regular meeting time. It can be by conference call, it can be by Skype or Zoom or what have you, and everybody should be committed to showing up on time and participating. It can't just be something that's treated like a casual engagement that you attend if you don't have some more pressing business to handle. It should be like a doctor's appointment. You wouldn't say to your dentist, "Well, you know, I was busy." You have an appointment and you're expected to show up.

If there are shared values, if there's a commitment to participation, and just one other person, you have a Master Mind group. Then, you can invite in other people as time passes and you'll be surprised when you do form your group, chances are as time goes on you will encounter people who tell you, "Hey, I'm looking to form a Master Mind group."

You and your other group members will have to decide, will this person be adding to the bonfire? Will this person be bringing logs to the fire? Because, you have to have people of similar values and to some degree, similar humor, tone, temperament. Group harmony is the vital ingredient. Napoleon Hill really emphasized that again and again. He was much less concerned with the mechanics of things like: Is the group more religious? Is the group more secular? Is the group more one way? Is the group more another way? How many people are in it?, and so on. He felt those details are all secondary, but the one absolute requirement is group harmony.

17

Your Imaginary Council

Someone on social media once told a member of my Master Mind group: "Napoleon Hill never had a Master Mind group. In *Think and Grow Rich*, he talked about an imaginary group of advisers."

Is this true, my colleague wondered?

Not exactly. It is a common misreading of a passage Hill wrote toward the end of the book. Hill did describe regularly convening an "imaginary council" of historical eminences from whom he received guidance, advice, and lessons in character building. But he never called that a substitute for a Master Mind group, for him or anyone else. Taken on its own terms, however, the imaginary council technique can be a useful and powerful augmentation to your program of success.

Hill described his imaginary council technique this way:

Long before I had ever written a line for publication, or endeavored to deliver a speech in
public, I followed the habit of reshaping my own
character, by trying to imitate nine men whose
lives and life-works had been most important
to me. These nine men were, Emerson, Paine,
Edison, Darwin, Lincoln, Burbank, Napoleon,
Ford, and Carnegie. I held an imaginary Council meeting with this group whom I called my
"Invisible Counselors."

The procedure was this. Just before going to
sleep at night, I would shut my eyes, and see in
my imagination, this group of men seated with
me around my Council Table. Here I had not
only an opportunity to sit among those whom I
considered to be great, but I actually dominated
the group, by serving as the Chairman.

If this kind of practice appeals to you and your
Master Mind group members, you can try it individu-
ally, perhaps taking turns and reporting back results to
your group. Hill reached some truly remarkable insights
through this imaginary group of advisers. For example, one evening when Hill relaxed into meditation
and began to imagine a meeting of his invisible advisers he had an experience with "Thomas Edison," which
helped clarify some of his metaphysics and views on the
extra-physical nature of the mind. Hill wrote:

One evening Edison arrived ahead of all the
others. He walked over and seated himself at my
left, where Emerson was accustomed to sit, and

said, "You are destined to witness the discovery of the secret of life. When the time comes, you will observe that life consists of great swarms of energy, or entities, each as intelligent as human beings *think* themselves to be. These units of life group together like hives of bees, and remain together until they disintegrate, *through lack of harmony.* These units have differences of opinion, the same as human beings, and often fight among themselves. These meetings which you are conducting will be very helpful to you. They will bring to your rescue some of the same units of life which served the members of your Cabinet, during their lives. These units are eternal. THEY NEVER DIE! Your own thoughts and DESIRES serve as the magnet which attracts units of life, from the great ocean of life out there. Only the friendly units are attracted— the ones which harmonize with the nature of your DESIRES."

The other members of the Cabinet began to enter the room. Edison got up, and slowly walked around to his own seat. Edison was still living when this happened. It impressed me so greatly that I went to see him, and told him about the experience. He smiled broadly, and said, "Your dream was more a reality than you may imagine it to have been." He added no further explanation to his statement.

I believe you should feel a great sense of creative license in devising your imaginary council. It can consist of several members or just one. It can take the form of an appeal to a Higher Power or deity. It is possible that prayer itself is energy personified, or that prayer is an operation in which the mind is personified as deity. This is productive and insightful whether or not you believe that humanity exists beyond its five senses. If you take a more materialist or secular view of life, then certain forms of meditative questioning can tap the depths of your psyche. Or, if you take a metaphysical approach, you can view such sessions as appeals to Infinite Intelligence, God, or whatever your conception of a greater power.

In 1895, William James made this important observation: "I confess that I do not see why the very existence of an invisible world may not in part depend on the personal response which any one of us may make to the religious appeal. God himself, in short, may draw vital strength and increase of very being from our fidelity." Consider the implications of James's statement. The philosopher is suggesting that your appeal to a Higher Power, Infinite Intelligence, or any aspect of an unseen world *may in itself strengthen the presence and experience of that unseen principle in your life.*

That may be what Hill was experiencing when he appealed to Infinite Intelligence in the figure of his imaginary advisers. I encourage you to experiment with this method, and allow it to develop along whatever lines are most compelling.

Action Step
Your Daily Seven

In addition to working with an "imaginary council" I want to share with you my seven daily practices. If done with commitment, these techniques will improve both your inner and outer life.

1. **Morning Connection**. Upon waking connect to your highest ideals—do this *before* picking up your phone or getting sucked into social media. Depending on your belief system, you can say The Lord's Prayer or repeat an affirmation while still in bed, such as: "Day by day, in every way, I am getting better and better." (For more on this mantra see chapter twelve, "Self-Help for the Secular." I also offer two favorite prayers in chapter twenty-three, "Why Self-Help Matters.")

2. **Sacred Literature**. Connect, however briefly, with a piece of ethical or religious literature. Even if it's just a single line from the Tao Te Ching, Book of Proverbs, or Bhagavad Gita, carry it in your mind. I am registered to receive a morning email passage from mystical teacher Vernon Howard (anewlife.org).

3. **Express Gratitude**. After actor Christopher Reeve was rendered quadriplegic in an equestrian accident, he observed: "I see somebody just get up out of a chair and stretch and I go, 'No, you're not even thinking about what you're doing and how

lucky you are to do that.'" Each morning enumerate at least three things for which you're grateful.

4. Three P.M. Prayer. Christ is said to have died on the cross at 3 p.m. I set a daily alarm on my phone for 3 p.m. Eastern to say a brief prayer for people who have written to me, or to ask for personal guidance or help.

5. Choose Kindness. Toward the end of his life, British intellectual and spiritual seeker Aldous Huxley was asked to name—out of all the vast philosophies he had experimented with—the single best method for inner development. "Just try being a little kinder," Huxley replied.

6. Radically Forgive. Commit daily to an authentic effort to forgive someone who has hurt you. (This doesn't necessarily mean allowing that person back into your life.) If you can honestly attempt this you will begin to experience a new sense of calm. Remember: *We become what we do not forgive.*

7. Reject Humiliation. Much of our social media, talk radio, and reality TV dishes out the cruel glee of witnessing people get humiliated. Avoid media that drags people through the mud. What if ten percent of the population took a "no humiliation" pledge? Be among that ten percent.

18

The Energy of Applied Faith

Although I am a spiritual person I have always had difficulty with the concept of faith. I've never quite been able to define it for myself. Is it hope? Persistence? Belief that the floorboards will appear as I take a step into the unknown?

Several years ago, I experienced a deep sense of sympathy when I learned from a clergyman that a world-famous colleague of his—a widely known minister who had written several bestsellers—was on his deathbed when the figure's daughter walked into an adjacent room where friends and family were gathered in vigil and she declared plaintively: "Daddy has no faith." Everyone was surprised and even shocked by her comment. When I heard the story I didn't judge this minister. I felt that I could be in a similar position myself someday.

Yet Napoleon Hill's work gave me a clearer, more workable definition of faith. Hill helped me to see what faith really is—and how its application can move you steadily toward your goals, and rescue you when you feel depressed, stuck, or lost. In *The Master Key to Riches*, Hill outlines nine qualities of constructive faith:

1. Definiteness of purpose supported by personal initiative and action.

2. The habit of going the extra mile in all human relationships.

3. A Master Mind alliance with one or more people who display courage and who are suited spiritually and mentally to your needs in carrying out a given purpose.

4. A positive mind avoidant of negatives, such as fear, envy, greed, hatred, jealousy, and superstition. (A Positive Mental Attitude, or PMA, is further discussed in the appendix.)

5. Recognition that every adversity carries with it the seed of equivalent benefit; that temporary defeat is *not* failure unless you define it as such.

6. The habit of affirming your Definite Major Purpose at least once daily in meditation.

7. Recognition of Infinite Intelligence, which gives orderliness to life. Hill taught that all of us are

minute expressions of this Intelligence; and, as such, the individual mind has no absolute limitations except those that are accepted and set up by the individual.

8. A careful inventory of your past defeats and adversities, which will reveal that all such experiences are instructive and can serve as springboards to new achievement.

9. Self-respect expressed through harmony with one's own conscience, ethics, and personal sense of fair play.

Having identified Hill's nine principles of faith, I want to expand on each and explore how you can use it. Now, in the first book in the Napoleon Hill Success Course series, *The Miracle of a Definite Chief Aim*, I wrote that I viewed faith as *persistence*. If you have difficulty with the term faith you can try substituting persistence and see what effect it has. That worked for me at the time. But today I have a broader view of faith, thanks to Hill. I believe that this exploration of his principles will show you why.

Definiteness of Purpose

Hill repeatedly emphasized, as I have in this book, the necessity of having a Definite Chief Aim. What does that have to do with faith? Since our emotions control so much of how we live, the very fact of selecting an aim for which you feel passion will consistently direct your energies—in a manner analogous to faith—toward your desire. We can repeat affirmations or maxims to ourselves that we do not believe or believe only intermittently, but we can never fool our emotions. This is why self-honesty is critical when selecting a workable, lifelong aim. If you truly know what you want, the force of your emotions will be at your back; this drives you forward in ways that you may not suspect—and instills you with a sense of faith that you are capable of arriving where you feel you must.

Going the Extra Mile

In earlier chapters I noted the corrosive habit of fecklessness and apathy in our culture. This problem touches almost every home, office, arts space, and institution. But if you routinely go the extra distance for someone, that person will not only recognize your distinction (and if he or she doesn't then you're in the wrong environment) but you will also believe more in yourself and in what you're capable of. Doing more than expected not only benefits those around you but also brings psychological benefits to you. Earned self-belief is a key facet of faith.

Master Mind Alliance

As explored in chapter sixteen, when you enter into a Master Mind group you benefit from the practical advice, collegiality, and moral support of all the members of your group. But something further is at work. Hill noted—and I have discovered this in my own experience—that an additional force settles over the proceedings of a harmonious Master Mind group. Each member, like marathon runners urged on by teammates, gains an added sense of energy, mental acuity, resolve, and enthusiasm. Hill considered this the benefits of Infinite Intelligence, a concept I expand on below. The Master Mind is Infinite Intelligence localized. This process can be described but it will do you no good until it is experienced through the workings of a Master Mind alliance.

Positive Mental Attitude (PMA)

I have a tattoo of a lightning bolt capped by the letters PMA inside my left bicep. My inspiration for this, both visually and spirituality, came from the pioneering punk band Bad Brains, who use this image as their logo. The band credits its success to *Think and Grow Rich* and PMA. Remember that whenever someone tries to stereotype motivational literature or positive thinking. This philosophy is for everyone. PMA does not mean cultivating fuzzy thoughts or trying to block out the tough realities of life. Not at all. It means believing in your own resources, inventiveness, and resilience as a sacred personal code. (Possessing a personal code is further explored in the following chapter.)

Learning from Adversity

In chapter ten I wrote that the principle of learning from failure "isn't some cloying bromide." That is a hard-won truth. The difference between giving up and pushing on—which is to say, possessing faith—rests largely in your ability to review setbacks or disappointments and to earnestly search for what such episodes can teach you. I have almost never failed to find a lesson in disappointment, even if the emotional sting lingers. Sometimes it takes me a week or more to get past the emotional letdown of a temporary failure. But when the setback occurs I immediately review what I can do better in future episodes. Did I overlook warning signs? Could I have been more patient in devising and presenting my plans or pitches? Did I do enough to accommodate the needs of the other people involved? Did I cut corners? These lessons drive you forward.

Daily Meditation

Sometimes we work so hard at empirical or outer tasks that we neglect our sense of larger vision. It is vital to pause at least once a day—and ideally more—to remind yourself of your aim and your ultimate destination. I have written my definite aim into a document and coupled it with a personal coat of arms, which a spiritual colleague created for me. Several times a day I stop what I am doing and revisit that written aim and image. I also think of my aim when I am drifting off to sleep at night and waking in the morning (a pillar of autosuggestion, as seen in chapter twelve). I meditate on my aim and visualize its achievement. Be sure that you never neglect vision and meditation; they are expressions and fortifications of faith.

Infinite Intelligence

Even if you are secular in your personal outlook there is no barrier to using Hill's philosophy. One of his foundational principles is that all people are inlets of Infinite Intelligence—a universal, non-localized intellect in which we all take part. The ancient Greeks called it *nous*. Ralph Waldo Emerson called it the Over-Soul. New Thought writers sometimes called it Infinite Mind. Whatever language you use, the principle is that Infinite Intelligence is a storehouse of intuition, insight, and epiphanies. Hill taught that our wellspring of intellect runs deeper and contains greater resources than we realize. In whatever way you approach the topic you may be assured that you possess fuller mental reserves than is apparent. Often these reserves reach you after dedicating yourself to a chosen task to the point of mental and physical exhaustion—and then taking a rest, or allowing yourself downtime, recreation, meditation, or a nap or night's sleep.

I discovered this when I was invited to deliver my first public lecture in fall of 2005. I sat awake in my Los Angeles hotel room not knowing how I would organize my thoughts into a cogent lecture the next day. I had already put in exhaustive preparation, but I remained unsure of how it all gelled. I decide to set aside my work and watch a movie to relax. About 45 minutes into Steven Spielberg's remake of *War of the Worlds*, I had a sudden insight as to how to organize my presentation. I turned off the movie and assembled my thoughts onto note cards. My outline not only formed the basis of a successful talk the following day, but it served as the skeleton for my first book, *Occult America*. I believe Hill would've described this episode as Infinite Intelligence in action. Use whatever language you like, but when you undergo this kind of experience it builds your faith that you are not without untapped resources.

Self-Inventory

This principle relates to the earlier observation about learning from setbacks or adversity. You must not flagellate yourself but at the same time must be starkly frank about identifying your weaknesses and strengths, and how they have played out in specific episodes. For example, one of my weaknesses is impatience. I sometimes expect people to respond more quickly than they are able, especially when my enthusiasm (which tends to be a strength) runs high-octane. I suspect that my trait of impatience has sometimes earned me "no's" that would've been "yes's" if only I could have been more patient and allowed another party the time needed to reflect on a pitch or a proposal. I believe this is a healthful act of self-inventory in the face of setback. This kind of exercise is always available to you. It will build your faith that you're not operating under star-crossed circumstances or bad luck, but that everything you do can be improved and strengthened.

Self-Respect

In all matters of business, Hill urged practices of plain dealing, transparency, and mutual benefit. You will not find a single word contradicting that in *Think and Grow*

Rich or any of Hill's work. Such practices not only give you a reputation for personal accountability, and thus help you attract collaborators, backers, and clients, but they also improve your sense of legitimate self-respect. Many people complain that they suffer from poor self-image or insecurities. Always remember that self-respect is conditioned not only by your early environment but also by your day-to-day conduct. Just one act of abstaining from gossip or trash talk, one act of taking the blame and making something right when it goes awry, or one act of going the extra distance for a customer or colleague helps you stand more fully erect internally, and probably externally too. When that occurs, you experience a sense of earned and valid self-respect. Other people read this self-respect in your character, consciously or not. This sense of self-respect not only makes you more personally magnetic but it creates a symbiosis of faith—both that which you have in yourself and that which others have in you.

In considering this list of principles, I hope you will begin to realize, as Hill intended, that *faith can be learned*. Faith is not a trait that you are necessarily born with or that reaches you in an epiphanic moment (although both of those things are possible). Rather, faith, like all of the traits in Hill's success program, can be learned through principle, experience, and action.

In the end, what is faith? It is knowing that what you see is not all there is. And that hidden resources are available to you in equal measure to the challenges you face—*provided you have worked to make them manifest.*

Action Step
Suffering and Motivational Thought

There are times in life when tragedy unavoidably falls upon us and shakes our sense of faith, hope, and possibility. This is as lawful as the setting of the sun. We can debate whether injustice, evil, or suffering are real in any ultimate sense, but in the world in which we dwell they are palpably felt.

Critics often, and not unfairly, say that motivational thinkers do not adequately address suffering. A public-radio host once asked me: If you were a metaphysical minister, what would you tell a congregant who had suffered a terrible tragedy or loss? I would refer to the words of Rabbi Joshua Loth Liebman (1907–1948), a pioneering self-help author and liberal Boston rabbi.

Liebman was loosely connected with an early twentieth-century movement called Jewish Science, which began as a theological alternative to Christian Science. Close in outlook to New Thought, Jewish Science carries on today with a congregation on Manhattan's eastside.

Liebman was one of the few leaders in the positive-mind movement who directly addressed the Holocaust. Two years after the war, the rabbi said:

Mine has been a rabbinate of trouble—of depression. Hitler's rise, world crisis, global war, the attempted extermination of my people . . .

For those who have lost loved ones during the tragic war, all of the rest of life will be but a half loaf of bread—yet a half loaf eaten in courage and accepted in truth is infinitely better than a moldy whole loaf, green with the decay of self-pity and selfish sorrow which really dishonors the memory of those who lived for our up building and happiness.

We honor life by valuing the sacrifices that others have made for us, and the opportunities we are granted for developing our highest potential. Recall the philosophical question that was posed earlier:

"What do you do when someone offers you a gift?"

"You accept it."

The continuation of one's life following a tragedy is to accept an irreplaceable gift. We have been given life for a purpose, which is: to be generative. Use your life. Go and build.

19

A Personal Code

Napoleon Hill wrote often of his heroes: Thomas Edison, Ralph Waldo Emerson, Abraham Lincoln, and Andrew Carnegie, among others. He venerated their achievements, practical ideas, and principles. Yet consider how rare it is today that any of us strive to live by an ideal, credo, or principle.

Most of the time we seek ways to win praise and security, particularly from peer groups that we want to enter or remain in. We go along, looking for whatever we believe we can realistically expect in terms of money, prestige, and approval.

I challenge you to an experiment that breaks with that approach to life.

Are you willing to dedicate nine months, the gestation period of a new life, to relinquishing your conventional sense of security, and redirecting your existence to a new, and possibly higher, principle—one of your own choosing?

First, I want you to select a book that expresses an ethical or spiritual outlook with which you passionately agree. Choose a work that has attained posterity, even if within a small circle, which confirms its pull on the moral imagination.

Your choice may be a sacred or ethical work such as the *Tao Te Ching, Bhagavad Gita, Upanishads, Ethics of the Fathers, Paradise Lost, Meditations of Marcus Aurelius,* or the *Beatitudes.* It may be a modern self-help book such as *Think and Grow Rich, Alcoholics Anonymous,* or Viktor Frankl's *Man's Search for Meaning.* Or it may be an artist's or philosopher's vision of the good life such as Ayn Rand's *Atlas Shrugged,* Thoreau's *Walden,* Nietzsche's *Beyond Good and Evil,* or Neville Goddard's *Resurrection.*

The core requirement is that your book must summon you to a deeply felt, intimate goal or sense of purpose. The only restriction is that your chosen work must not require you to denigrate or obstruct another person's search or striving for his own highest potential.

At the back of your choice should be the perennial questions: What do I want? How do I want to live?

Then, dedicate yourself to your book and its ideas with unreserved passion for nine months.

I recommend not discussing what you're doing with anyone, with exceptions for members of a trusted support group, such as a twelve-step or Master Mind alliance. This is so you feel no pressure to submit your choices to the judgment of others, who may not share or understand your values.

I mentioned earlier that the spiritual teacher Jiddu Krishnamurti taught that the biggest barrier to creativity and personal excellence is seeking out and clinging to respectability. This is one of the maladies of modern life. We nest within our own subcultures and their attendant social and news media. We repeat what we're supposed to want, or what we claim to value, often (and sometimes subtly) parroting what we think makes us look good to others. We stand for nothing. Hence, we never realize what we're capable of.

Are you willing to risk all that for nine months?

In committing to an ethical idea, you must also be willing for your idea to be wrong. If through experience your selected idea proves faulty or false that forms a steppingstone in your search for truth. And if it proves right, you are delivered to a higher state of conduct, from which to continue your search.

You will find that your mind or energies often drift away from your core principle over the course of nine months. That is unavoidable. Our minds are undisciplined and our emotions routinely steal away our intentions. When that occurs, do not worry or handwring; just make an effort to return your attention to your book and its principles. Even the difficulty of holding to your ideals can itself become a self-revealing experience if you watch for it.

You will also be faced with the challenge of *acting* on your ideals. This will be a very personal matter—and it may be fraught with trial and error. There is no parable of heroism in which the protagonist is not plagued with doubt and misstep. This is part of an effort to do more than function within convention. Allow yourself to stumble during these nine months. One act of authentic self-determination can prove more fortifying than a string of missteps.

Think how wonderful it would be to invest yourself fully in one ideal. The very act of living for something immediately gives you an improved sense of self-possession and purpose. You experience the sensation of being "consciously right, superior, and happy," as William James put it. You are set apart.

Action Step
Rediscovering a Magical Book

The short book called *The Kybalion*, published in 1908, is, in my view, one of the most important metaphysical works of the twentieth century. If you haven't read it, or if the mysterious book has fallen off your radar, you may benefit from exploring it, as I did during one meaningful summer, where I reread it multiple times.

The Kybalion is authored by "Three Initiates," which was one of several pseudonyms used by Chicago publisher, lawyer, and New Thought visionary William Walker Atkinson (1862–1932), whom historical and documentary sources pinpoint as the work's sole author. Unveiling the mystery of the book's authorship in no way detracts from its scope and achievement.

The greatness of *The Kybalion* is that Atkinson successfully captured—and made relevant for modern seekers—facets of the late-ancient Greek-Egyptian philosophy called Hermeticism. The Hermetic texts, or Hermetica, explore existential, magical, alchemical, and occult ideas, and formed an essential part of the Renaissance outlook (the period in which they were rediscovered), and also influenced elements of scientific and rational thought associated with the Age of Enlightenment.

The value of *The Kybalion* is that Atkinson expertly and artfully summarized the metaphysical psychology of some of the Hermetic works, and married it to his considerable insights into modern New Thought.

Hermeticism is not exactly the religious ancestor to New Thought or mind-power metaphysics. Early New Thoughters were largely independent investigators who reached their insights about the mind's causative abilities chiefly through self-experiment. But aspects of Hermeticism *do* represent a distant historical parallel to New Thought, especially its core idea that a Great Mind of Creation brought all things into being, and that this same creative mental faculty dwells in all people.

"... your mind is god the father; they are not divided from one another for their union is life," says the Hermetica. (I am quoting from Brian P.

Copenhaver's translation.) This statement would be at home in any New Thought book.

If it were somehow possible for contemporary metaphysical seekers to reach back in time and have an exchange with the ancient Hermeticists, something like *The Kybalion* is probably as good an estimate as we have of what would appear.

20

What Emerson Understood

I previously mentioned that Napoleon Hill considered Transcendentalist philosopher Ralph Waldo Emerson (1803–1882) one of his personal heroes. Hill quotes Emerson more than any other philosopher. Part of Emerson's greatness as a writer, and the reason he won the lifelong admiration of Hill and many others, is that he never shied away from practicality. This was also true of Emerson's philosophical descendant William James, who is as much a hero to me as Emerson was to Hill.

It can be argued that Emerson's most practical works, which include essays such as *Power, Wealth*, and *Fate*, were not among his greatest. Critic Irving Howe wrote that in such works the philosopher "merely tugs the complexities... into the shallows of the explicit." There is truth in this charge. And yet this judgment fails to take account of Emerson's bravery. Emerson felt obligated to be direct—to provide his readers with actual plans of action. If this approach reduced his philosophical heights it also banished authorial cowardice. Emerson would not dodge the question of *how* to attempt the kind of self-directed living that his essays extolled.

In particular, the essays *Power* and *Wealth*, which Emerson published in his collection *The Conduct of Life* in 1860, prescribe the philosopher's view of how and under what conditions a person can successfully assert his will in life.

In *Power*, Emerson names four essential elements to exercising personal power. The first—and that which sustains all the others—is to be "in sympathy with the course of things." Echoing Taoism and other Eastern philosophies, Emerson believed that an individual could read the *nature of things* and seek to merge with it, like a twig carried downstream. "The mind that is parallel with the laws of nature," he writes, "will be in the current of events, and strong with their strength."

The second element of power is *health*. Emerson means this on different levels. He is speaking broadly of the vitality of body and spirit; the state of physicality and personal morale that sustains risks, seeks adventure, and completes plans. But he also speaks of routine bodily health, without which the individual's energies are sapped.

The third element is *concentration*. One of nature's laws is that concentration of energies brings impact. The concentration of a striking blow delivers the greatest force. Too often we deplete our energies by dispersing or spreading thin our aims and efforts. In *Power*, an imaginary oracle says: "Enlarge not thy destiny, endeavor not to do more than is given thee in charge." Like light focused in a laser, concentration into a single channel, task, or aim brings you the greatest power.

The fourth and final element is *drilling*. By this, Emerson means rehearsing a practice over and over until you can perform it with osmotic excellence. The martial artist repeats his movements and routines to the point where they enter his physical memory and are available under all conditions. Likewise, we must drill, practice, or rehearse—to the point where we have unconsciously mastered our task or specialty.

In his essay *Wealth*, Emerson declares, chin out, that the individual is "born to be rich." And by riches, the philosopher is not employing a coy metaphor. He means what he says. In a 2019 interview, a *New York Times* reporter asked performer Barry Manilow: "Would you have been happier playing piano in a jazz group?" The pop star replied: "Happier? I like the house and the Range Rover. I love the way I live." Emerson probably would have admired the performer's candor.

But the philosopher also identifies accumulation of capital as *befitting only that person who uses it to productive ends*. Emerson continues,

> Every man is a consumer, and ought to be a pro-
> ducer. He fails to make his place good in the
> world, unless he not only pays his debt, but also
> adds something to the common wealth. Nor
> can he do justice to his genius, without making

some larger demand on the world than a bare subsistence. He is by constitution expensive, and needs to be rich.

Only those purchases that expand your power and abilities, Emerson writes, leave you any richer. Indeed, wealth that fails to accompany expansion is wealth thrown away. "Nor is the man enriched," Emerson writes, "in repeating the old experiments of animal sensation." Rather, you are enriched when you increase your ability to earn, to do, and to grow. Wealth, properly understood, is power. That is why these essays are conjoined in this chapter.

So, how do you earn wealth? Emerson outlines roughly three steps: 1) First filling some nonnegotiable, subsistence-level need in your own life: this what drove the primeval farmers, hunter-gathers, and early villagers. 2) Next, applying one's particular talents to nature, and expansively filling the needs of others. If you do not know or understand your talents, you must start there before anything is possible. Your talent is a potential source of excellence. And, finally, 3) using your wealth for the purpose of productiveness: paying down debts, making compound investments, and procuring the tools of your trade. Building and expanding is the only sound way to riches. And such things also reflect your code and nature as a progressing being.

By bowing to the mechanics of practicality, did Emerson sacrifice some of his transcendental splendor? Some thought so; I see it differently. If Emerson had avoided such an approach he would have been guilty of failing to take his philosophy to the streets. Complexity does not excuse inaction. And here I am reminded of an observation by the flawed but brilliant poet Ezra Pound: "But to have done instead of not doing/This is not vanity."

Action Step
Emerson as Self-Help

Ralph Waldo Emerson can and should be read as self-help. He intended his essays to be discussed and acted upon by the broadest-possible sector of the seeking public.

Years ago when I was in publishing, I assembled a short anthology of some of Emerson's most powerful writings. The book included an excellent brief introduction by a scholar I admired. The collection grew popular and gave me a great deal of personal satisfaction. But one precinct wasn't happy. An academic newsletter dedicated to the study of Emerson panned the book in a review. The reviewer, a professor of English literature, bemoaned the anthology's absence of bibliographical material and historical notes.

On the first count, the critic was inattentive: a page of bibliographical material appeared at the end of the book. In terms of the other complaint about the absence of historical or analytical notes, he was right. No notes appeared. I considered them unnecessary, and, in fact, viewed such an addition as a hindrance to the reader's experience.

I believe that many of today's reprints of classic literature are weighted down with excessive prefatory material and notes. I asked the writer of the introduction to limit himself to a concise and practical introduction, which he did admirably. I wanted the motivated reader to move into Emerson's writing with as little barrier as possible. The professor saw things differently. "It is impossible," he wrote, "to understand Emerson without historical notes." His statement shocked me, and still does. It showed disrespect for the reader. What would Emerson have said? The philosopher delivered public lectures, which he expeditiously issued as pamphlets or articles to circulate his ideas as broadly as possible among the reading public. William James, who was in some ways Emerson's inheritor, followed the same practice.

To maintain that a great work—whether an essay, opera, play, or philosophical tract—can be engaged or understood solely with the annotation of an acknowledged expert is to degrade the bond between artist and audience. I am not antagonistic toward historical or analytic notes; they contribute value to many works and are a necessary aspect of scholarship. But to treat them as a tollgate to entry, without which understanding is considered "impossible," denigrates the value of the individual search. This type of attitude fuels the public's not-always-unwarranted wariness toward academia.

Philosophers are not specialists. Lasting philosophers are teachers of ideas. This is why William James, in a talk delivered at UC Berkeley in 1898, bemoaned the rise of scholastic philosophy, and instead called for a public philosophy that demonstrated "*cash-value*, in terms of particular experience." (His emphasis appeared in the original). Emerson called for a "philosophy for the people."

In addition to the essays mentioned in this chapter, I recommend that you read Emerson's *Self-Reliance*; *The Over-Soul*; *Circles*; *Spiritual Laws*; *Success*; and *Compensation*. You will probably find, as I have, the temptation to highlight and underline passage after passage. These works supply a wealth of actionable wisdom. Make no mistake: they are self-help. If you have any doubts, you'll see in my final chapter that Emerson himself coined the term "self-help."

21

Think and Grow Rich:
Challenges and Responses

In 2018, I delivered a workshop in Denver on how to work with *Think and Grow Rich* in today's world. One evening, the participants asked some very probing and challenging questions. I share the best of them here. These are the kinds of questions that transcend mere commentary or a request for rote answers. These questions transform a workshop into a true exchange and a shared search between speaker and attendees. The questions and my responses are slighted edited for flow or clarity, and otherwise appear as they occurred that night.

Q: *I read* Think and Grow Rich *when I was in my twenties and I couldn't resonate with it at all. I was completely unambitious, never had any goals. I've never had a burning desire in my life for anything on any level. It just isn't part of my nature, my makeup. So I couldn't get through the book. I thought, well this is for some people. Something that did strike me, and this is what I want to ask you about, is that what seemed to be missing from it and a lot of these books, was what I saw as trust. Because I do sleep at night, and I have done a lot and life has been great and stuff, but it all came through trusting. So instead of setting goals and worrying whether, "Have I got a Master Mind? Have I got this?" I was just saying, "I'm here; I wouldn't be here unless you wanted me to do something."*

And whenever something happened that I was needed for, something or somebody would come to me out of the blue, or a phone would ring and go, "We need you to do this," and I'd go, "Okay." So that to me was all accomplished without goal-setting and striving and desires. I committed to trusting. It was the only commitment I've really ever made. I committed just to trusting.

I trusted that if I was here, I was needed. And if I was needed, I would say yes to what I was meant to do and see where it got me.

So my question is, are the two concepts mutually exclusive in your head, or in this book and in this field, or can people just relax? Say you had not done what you'd done, and you chose to sleep and you chose to just do whatever you do, and not try so hard with your Master Mind or whatever, would you have been just as successful? Obviously you'd be just as intelligent and just as smart, but would you have got where you wanted to go without all the effort?

A: That is a wonderful question, and I have seriously and intently wrestled with that. I guess I would have to say I came to the place where I am right now because of my own internal wrestling with that question. This is the form that my wrestling took. For a long time, I was dedicated to two different spiritual teachers and two different spiritual outlooks. I'll mention the names just in case anybody's interested in them. They have lots of published works and they're easy to find. Both men are deceased.

One was a teacher named Vernon Howard, who was a very beautiful, very unclassifiable metaphysical teacher who died in 1992. Vernon described exactly what you are articulating. His was a system of radical trust, of *just be*. There was a quality of the Tao in Vernon. There was a quality of primeval Christianity in Vernon. He taught that we are clothed like lilies of the field, and I felt and I knew in my heart that Vernon possessed great, great truth. He had kind of a stern style sometimes, but everything he was saying was a very direct echo of what you've annunciated, and it was a very beautiful, primeval spiritual approach of an exquisite trust.

The other spiritual teacher, whose work and ideals I was very attached to, and remain so, was Neville Goddard, a beautiful teacher who was, loosely speaking, from the New Thought tradition. He passed on in 1972, so they're both modern teachers, but not contemporary to us. Neville's teaching was essentially that desire is sacred, and your imagination is God and your intellect out-pictures everything that you experience, and that Scripture, both Old Testament and New Testament, is simply an allegory of your mind as God the Creator. And Neville would say, in effect, "my words are rooted in you." Everything that you experience is actually a creation of your own intellect. Your imagination is God in the most literal sense. As such, your desires and your impulses and that for which you're reaching is sacred, is beautiful, is an act of creation every bit as exquisite as anything recounted in the book of Genesis, which Neville would say is an allegory for your own imagination.

I found myself completely divided between these two approaches, because I think they are different. I have friends in the New Thought world who insist to me, "No, it's all the *Tao Te Ching*," and so forth, and I'm not sure that's true at all. I think in actuality New Thought is an aspirational spirituality, and we like to say, "Thy will be done," as a principle, but it does measure things in a kind of before and after.

I came to feel that my approach, personally speaking, was Neville's approach—that our desires are sacred; that we are at our highest not only in trusting but in aspiring, in creating. I came to believe in the aspirational approach. I do think it's different, although God knows we fall to our knees in front of the mystery that life is. And I think there must be a convergence of all things if we're all emanating from one point of creation. There are lots of mitigating factors, but I guess I would have to say these are different roads to Rome. They both may be leading to Rome, but they are different roads and I came to feel that as much as I love Vernon, and I truly, truly believe in the validity and truth of his vision, my path is the aspirational path. In all honesty, I wouldn't sleep at night anyway, I suspect. I think that part of my freneticness is what naturally directed me towards the aspirational path. It may be that we as individuals have feet in both worlds. None of us can decide, "I owe nothing to the transcendent. I only live in the world of

Caesar," and none of us can decide, "I owe nothing to the world of Caesar, I only live in the transcendent." I think there must be some ultimate convergence, but I did come myself to the path of aspiration.

I thank you for that question; I try to respond to it with as much sincerity as I can.

Q: *As a transplant from another country into America, what I notice very much is that everybody is striving because they're all striving to make good, to own, to have, and so on because that's the breeding you have in America. I just wonder whether if they didn't try, and weren't going looking for what everybody else has and deciding, "Oh well, yes, we should have that too," and rather they just fell back a little bit more on their, let's say "divine programming," they might actually, not necessarily get further, but get as far in a more harmonious, rested, satisfied state than the anger, and frustration, and jealousy that comes from feeling you haven't got the right kind of car that the next guy has. That's purely sort of an outside observer's view of America. What do you think?*

A: I do understand that and I think a lot about that myself. It's an interesting question. I think every spiritual outlook, to some greater or lesser degree, reflects the time and place in which it was written. I do wonder whether some of the ethics of non-attachment and non-identification that one finds in Vedic and Buddhist literature also have something to do with that literature having been produced in societies that were profoundly stratified, and in some cases remain so. And that this vision, magnificent as it is, also addressed itself to some of the social realities that had existed for generations, and would exist for generations into the future, which the individual had to deal with. I sometimes observe that Western folk and Americans in particular have tremendous difficulty, almost constitutionally, with teachings of non-attachment and non- identification. I often find myself seeing that for many Americans, many American seekers, those teachings could almost tear them in two. It's very difficult constitutionally for some of us in the West to aspire in that way; that without the satisfaction of some kind of personal expression it's difficult for life to be a happy place.

You're raising a very, very good question and it's a challenging question. Again, I'll share one quick story and it doesn't resolve any of this, but if anything maybe it deepens our question as to what is the natural state of being human.

Years ago, I was in a very rigorous group dedicated to the study of esoteric ideas, and we would hold group meetings. There was a woman at one of these group meetings one winter, who said, almost in a manner of confession, that she had created an ice sculpture outside her house, and she was very proud of this ice sculpture that she had created, and she had some friends coming to visit her in the afternoon. It was a warming winter's day, and the sun was starting to come out, and she realized that the sun was going to melt her ice sculpture before her friends came to visit. She was saying to the group in tones of confession that she noticed, as she put it, her own ego at work, wanting her friends to hurry up and get there and see her beautiful ice sculpture before the afternoon sun took it away.

There was a very somber mood in the room after this woman had told this story, as if something had been confessed and shared. I thought to myself, I don't think that one needs to hide one's light under a bushel. She created something beautiful, and to wish for a constituency to see that work of beauty that she created, which I couldn't have created, seemed natural to me inasmuch as a farmer wants his crop yield to be good in a certain season. I didn't think there was something from the perspective of ego that this woman had to confess. It seemed to me that what she did was beautiful; and part of our expressiveness in the world, part of our creation of beauty or anything else that's productive in the world, is the wish for a constituency, or an artist wishing for an audience. An idea will wither without a constituency, hence we have Christ speaking on a mountaintop. We have Christ saying, go out to the highways and hedges and bring them in. I thought she created something beautiful. It seemed very natural to me.

Again, I don't know if that perspective is conditioning, or if it taps something that's primal to our human situation.

Q: You've brought up this "Thy will, my will" thing a couple of times throughout this series. I've wrestled with this a lot over the last year. I think it's important to highlight, hopefully you agree with this, that "thy will" isn't something out there that is telling you what to do. I don't know. What I've come to is that "thy will" is my higher-consciousness self at work when I'm paying attention to it and I think sometimes "thy will" is the place where we get afraid of the growing edge, then we get to step into that, but I'm curious, about your wrestling, because I've certainly had some.

A: Yeah. It's a current wrestling match. It's related to the question we were just exploring: is there a division between "Thy will be done," and "my will be done?"

If there's no God out there, isn't "my will, thy will; thy will, my will?" But then there's something higher calling, always.

It's a very big question. The path I've chosen at this point in my life as a seeker is that human desire is sacred, and there is a distinction that can be made between an ethical aspiration versus a violent aspiration. A violent aspiration being one that seeks to curtail another individual's pursuit of his or her own highest aspiration. Of course we stumble into problems and frictions due to lack of perspective, but at the same time, I do believe there are periods of profound sensitivity in people's lives where we do have higher perspective. It may not be the highest, but we do have higher perspective.

I've found that very often at intense moments of grief and intense moments of joy, sometimes people's social conditioning gets shut down and elements of higher perspective emerge. It could be that "thy will be done" is a statement that refers to both the beyond and the internal, if I can put it that way, simultaneously when we have these moments of exquisite awareness. I think they may come intermittently, they may not always be consistent, and there may be things that interrupt them all the time, but they are there. At such times I think that there may be one will that can be spoken of.

Q: *I'm struck with the fact that you continue to reference a lot of male authors, and obviously that's a part of our world, but our world is transitioning. Can you share with us some of the female authors that you've read or that you would invite us to be inspired with as women start to emerge more in leadership in the New Thought movement?*

A: Oh sure. I'm deeply admiring of Florence Scovel Shinn, of course the author of *The Game of Life*, who I think was one of the great voices of the new metaphysics in the early twentieth century. Actually, I dedicate *The Miracle Club* to Helen Wilmans, the author of *The Conquest of Poverty*, her great book from 1899, and I write about Wilmans as well in my book *One Simple Idea* because I view her as one of the great voices that sort of married the new metaphysics, by which I mean New Thought and Christian Science, and some of the associated philosophies, with a progressive political vision. That, of course, is part of the untold history of New Thought.

I write about that a lot in my books *Occult America* and *One Simple Idea*. There was this incredible marriage in America, which is just misunderstood, between the political avant-garde and the spiritual avant-garde. By the mid-nineteenth century, Spiritualists, and New Thoughters, and mental healers, and abolitionists, and suffragists, and early black nationalists, and all kinds of folks who believed in an ideal of political liberation, were united and they shared newspapers, newsletters, and meeting halls, and so on. Helen Wilmans was an author for a labor newspaper, and she eventually grew very frustrated with the fact that she felt the labor movement was doing all kinds of things in terms of passing of legislation and collective bargaining that were necessary, but was not addressing what she saw as the root crisis of the human condition. She wrote in one of her articles, in effect, "The problem with the working man today is that he will not think." She insisted that you had to combine a program of political liberation with the kind of internal searching and mind causation that we've been talking about.

I'm also greatly admiring of Elizabeth Towne, who was a suffragist activist, and who published one of the longest-running magazines in American history, *Nautilus*, which she founded at the turn of the century. It continued to publish through the mid-1950s. Towne was one of the early activists who helped to formulate the first presidential campaigns of Teddy Roosevelt, who was considered a very progressive candidate early in his career. She also became the first female town alderman in the town of Holyoke, Massachusetts, where she was from. She ran a campaign to become mayor of Holyoke, Massachusetts. Came in second. Towne was also a formative publisher who discovered Wallace D. Wattles, author of *The Science of Getting Rich*, and many other motivational greats.

Action Step
What is the Right Way to Affirm?

At workshops and online, people frequently ask me about the right way to use affirmations. Should affirmations be rendered in the present tense ("I am") or future tense ("I will")? Some argue that the future tense pushes off your aims to an unrealized point in time, and perpetuates current circumstances. Many people wonder: How should I structure my affirmations?

In actuality, I think this topic has been needlessly muddled by teachings that endorse programmatic consistency when harnessing the mind's creative properties.

The truth is: You should employ whatever language feels most authentic and natural, and helps sustain your emotive passion. If you have difficulty believing that you possess something right now, and it feels more persuasive to locate it in the future, then do so. May traditionalists forgive me: There is no wrong way of enunciating a goal.

The life of groundbreaking science-fiction novelist Octavia Butler (1947–2006) provides a case in point. Butler grew up in a working-class, African-American household in Pasadena, California, in the 1950s and 60s. Awkward, shy, and unusually tall for her age, Butler felt isolated from other kids. In her solitude, she developed voracious reading habits, and a burning desire to write. Butler went on to become sci-fi's first widely recognized African-American woman writer, winning popularity and critical acclaim.

Archivists at the Huntington Library in Los Angeles discovered among the novelist's papers an extraordinary and foresightful rendering of her personal vision, which Butler handwrote in 1988 in New Thought tones: "I shall be a bestselling writer... This is my life. I write bestselling nov-els... I will find the way to do this. So be it! See to it!" Butler freely used both future and present tenses in her vision. She wrote out her feelings without getting distracted by form.

Butler's manifesto expressed another positive-mind principle: purposeful success. "I will send poor black youngsters to... writer's workshops. I will help poor black youngsters broaden their horizons... I will get the best of health care for my mother and myself."

You can examine Butler's affirmation for yourself online, including at her Wikipedia page. Memorize it. Let its power permeate your psyche. Notice how a great artist understood that there are no wrong ways to express the vision of your desire.

22

Your Definite Chief *Weakness*

I have written and spoken a great deal about Napoleon Hill's principle of selecting a Definite Chief Aim. I consider it the single most important part of his program. But here we are turning it inside-out and asking: what is your definite chief weakness?

The intention is not to dwell on the underside of life but rather to become more self-aware, in the same way that Hill urges with his extensive character-assessment questionnaire in *Think and Grow Rich*. I believe that if you can honestly face your definite weakness, such an awareness can, in time, work as much of a revolution in your life as the selection of a Definite Chief Aim.

But let me caution you: our weaknesses are generally emotional in nature—often based in fear or hostility (which are largely the same)—and *self-awareness is only one part* of coming to terms with how a definite chief weakness disables or detracts from your life. Emotional reactions are very difficult to change, even with awareness. Identifying a trauma, the goal of most traditional therapy (though the field is trending toward behavioral-altering cognitive treatments), is important in itself; but the intellectual act, however insightful, is not necessarily cathartic. Not infrequently, the seeker can feel that the "root cause" has been identified (and there are sometimes several) but the problem persists.

This happened to me during the course of five years of psychoanalysis. I deeply respect the principle of psychoanalysis and how it seeks to fully unpeel the onion of human nature. But intensive talk-therapy can also, in my experience, leave the individual perpetually repeating and reviewing his or her past experiences and present schisms without producing change. This is because our emotions possess a life of their own, and they can be intensively running away even as the intellect is trying to assert a rationalistic viewpoint. Never conflate thoughts and emotions. They operate on different tracks. And emotions are more powerful: as a great teacher once said, pitting thoughts against emotions is like pitting steam power against nuclear power; the latter will win every time.

I know an excellent psychologist who implicitly recognizes this by telling patients: "Trauma is not what happens to you; it's what you do with what happens to you." He challenges patients to create a constructive reaction and counterpoint to the suffering they have experienced. The creation of a positive response-behavior does not immediately or altogether curtail the difficult emotional response; but over time it can supplant its primacy. Your constructive compensatory behavior, if it helps others and helps you, can make you nobler and stronger.

In asking you to probe your definite chief weakness, I am asking you to face yourself bluntly and honestly. In that vein, and as someone who sees himself as a seeker on the path with you, I will disclose to you my own definite chief weakness. It is paranoia. Not the kind of paranoia that runs toward conspiracy theories or hidden plots, which I eschew. Rather, my emotional paranoia works this way: If I do not hear back from someone in what I deem to be a timely way, I get nervous that something is wrong; that a plan, project, or relationship is fraying. Believe me, seeker to seeker, person to person—and I feel I owe you honest disclosure—I have wasted a lot of energy over the course of many years on these baseless fears. Such fears can invite a negative outcome. (One of the mysteries of human nature is that avoidance produces the very thing we seek to flee from.) Yet I must also note that there is an upside to this emotional reactiveness insofar as I often have a "plan B." That is, I foresee pitfalls in the road—real or imagined—and attempt to avert or navigate them. I have a backup plan. This has, on occasion, significantly aided me.

I suspect, but do not know, that my fears have something to do with an incomplete emotional connection in childhood. I was raised by a parent who often took pleasure in pushing my emotional buttons. This problem was worsened by the denial that this behavior was occurring. But even if I were certain that that cycle produced my chief weakness, I don't believe that that intellectual insight alone would fix the problem. Hence, I must continually labor to keep this emotional trait of heightened alarm in check.

I often counter this trait by seeking solutions and productive information in ways that do not necessarily resolve the root problem but that do allow me to function in optimal ways. Again, this otherwise difficult trait also pushes me to create backup plans. Such plans can come in handy. "Every stick has two ends," a great man once observed. Such is the case with your weakness. A weakness is the polarity of a strength—it can reflect a corresponding strength within you depending upon how you approach it. This is another reason why it's important to identify your chief weakness. By searching for positive, compensatory counter-behaviors you may naturally locate the strength that is the complement or polarity of your weakness.

One way to identify your definite chief weakness is to imagine what *others* would describe it as. You may want to ask them. What would your spouse, officemate, or best friend say? Do you erupt in anger? Subtly express judgments of others? Devise ways to put another in a "one down" position? Give your word and then break it (perhaps passively)? These traits can make a person difficult to work and live with. If any of them seem personally familiar they have probably limited some of your relationships and collaborations. In the long run, we get the company we deserve.

We can be chronically blind to our worst traits. I once knew a writer who would press people for details of their private lives—acting as a sympathetic confessor—and would later subtly, but unmistakably, use those details against them. Everyone saw it. He never did. Eventually the field of people who would work with this person narrowed. Hence, you may need to have a manipulative or damaging character trait pointed out to you. If you are willing to face it, that is.

Your willingness to consider your chief flaw indicates a great deal about your dedication to self-improvement. The path of self-help is noble and crucial. It is the whole point of this book—and this path is deeply worthy of a lifetime of effort, a principle to which we now, in closing, turn.

Action Step
Positive Thinking and the "Shadow"

I am sometimes asked about positive thinking and the "shadow." By shadow I mean the side of yourself that you do not always want to acknowledge. Carl Jung defined the shadow as the repository of your unspoken desires, fears, impulses, and yearnings. It may also be a place of unrealized abilities and personal powers.

Critics say that self-helpers or positive thinkers deny the shadow. Is that so?

Frankly, I don't see a conflict. As noted, to understand what you want in life, you must be fearlessly, even uncomfortably, honest with yourself. We are sometimes taught that our desires are ignoble, yet we also live in a society that encourages them—this can create a sense of internal conflict which follows us throughout adulthood. What were your *earliest* desires? What did you dream of and envision as a child that you never shared with anyone? Write it down privately. This kind of exercise, when done with maturity and absolute self-disclosure, can place you in touch with the part of your psyche known as the shadow.

Before you can arrive at a definite aim in life, and pursue what really matters to you, it is vital to know what dwells within every fold of your psyche. Years ago, someone who I believe possessed an authentic intuitive gift told me that my truest desire was for "power." She said I had an "over-developed superego." I was uncomfortable with her observations. For years I tried to push them away. I saw power-seekers as narrow, selfish, and aggressive.

As time passed, however, I was compelled to acknowledge the truth of what she said. This meant facing my shadow. In doing so, I learned that I did not want power in some violent or ugly manner. I didn't want to step on people or tells others what to do. Nor did I want to run a big office or anything like that. I wanted the kind of power that comes with personal agency—with the ability to frame and carry out my plans in life, while also being loyal, sensitive, and decent to people close to me.

I sometimes say that positive thinking is really *deliberative thinking*. The fullest expression of positivity is not picturing rosy tomorrows or dwelling on sunny thoughts, but rather knowing what you truly want, and using your mind's fullest constructive and causative abilities to move toward it. This requires probing every part of yourself—including the shadow.

23

Why Self-Help Matters

Napoleon Hill has inspired a great deal of what I've written in this book. He is without question one of the most influential self-help writers in modern history. I want to make my final observation about the power and nobility of continually seeking to improve yourself through his methods and others in the self-help field.

Some people today are turned off by self-help. The genre has developed a bit of a dowdy reputation. I was recently corresponding with a successful self-help writer who seemed embarrassed by the term.

"I don't see myself as a self-help writer," he explained. "I think that most self-help is a sham." The same writer later sent me a mass mailing for a "Magic Income Trick."

I know a bestselling writer of popular psychology who also rejects the label self-help because, she says, "I don't provide answers."

Why do good writers flee from a label that obviously belongs to them? Probably because they fear it's undignified. To some, it seems naïve or squishy. To others, self-help is gauche or down-market.

I feel the opposite. I believe that literate people should embrace the term self-help. I do.

Although I write as both a historian and a spiritual seeker, I wear the label proudly. Some of my books in the Napoleon Hill Success Course series are about finding a sense of purpose in life, or experimenting with the metaphysical properties of the mind or, like this one, cultivating personal habits that produce success. If I'm not a self-help writer—what am I?

The term self-help came into popular use in 1859, when British political reformer Samuel Smiles published his landmark work *Self-Help*, which celebrated good character, self-education, and accountability. Tame-sounding ideas today, but the profundity of simple ideas is revealed only in their application. The individual's struggle—or failure—to apply basic principles can place him before vast questions. Smiles' book became one of the most influential of its time.

Smiles did not coin the phrase self-help. As mentioned earlier, the term originated with Ralph Waldo Emerson. It appeared in Emerson's 1841 lecture, "Man the Reformer," a work that Smiles admired. "Can we not learn the lesson of self-help?" Emerson asked. "Society is full of infirm people, who incessantly summon others to serve them."

Emerson was *not* referring to the destitute, but rather to those who clamor for life's luxuries even while producing little themselves. By contrast, Emerson asked:

"Can anything be so elegant as to have few wants and to serve them one's self, so as to have somewhat left to give, instead of being always prompt to grab?"

Authentic self-help demands personal excellence; the drive to overcome addiction or crippling habits; and the wish to make life a little better for those who venture near us.

Some of the greatest exponents of self-help include therapist and Holocaust survivor Viktor Frankl; Alcoholics Anonymous cofounder Bill Wilson; and Emerson himself, who intended his essays as practical philosophy. Although the term didn't exist in his day, Benjamin Franklin can be considered a self-help writer for his popular tracts on good conduct. ("Early to bed and early to rise...")

The perpetually controversial Jordan Peterson is a self-help writer—and is misunderstood, in part, for that reason. I am interested in Peterson less because of his too-ready critique of Marxism and deconstructionism, but rather because his personal advice takes a back-to-basics approach to ethics, which can greatly aid the everyday individual and serve as a stabilizing force in life. *New York Times* columnist David Brooks runs down Peterson's self-empowerment program, such as personal accountability and desisting from lying, writing that it "sounds to me like vague exhortatory banality." Again, this is the conundrum of mistaking simplicity for triteness. The act of applying a single principle of self-elevation to your life is challenging—and filled with possibilities.

For example, I often tell people that one of the simplest and most powerful steps you can take to ennoble yourself and develop a sense of deserved self-esteem is to abstain from gossip and trash talk. When done for entertainment value, gossip and rumor-mongering are poison whose act engages you in perpetuating false-hoods and half-truths. Spreading or listening to hearsay degrades you in ways deeper than realized: consider how fitful, anxious, and physically depleted you feel after spending an hour gossiping. You are skittish because you have degraded another while failing to salve your own wounds. The gossiper implicitly, and wrongly, assumes that exposing another person's problems and weaknesses will dilute his or her own. Instead, you pierce the reputation of another—rarely knowing the full truth—which instigates a sense of guilt, and enacts the same values in you.

I am not talking about calling out injustices or objecting to abuse. Rather, I am talking about our chit-chat and media culture, which places a high premium on smears. Consider how much of our entertainment, such as reality television, centers on seeing other people humiliated. Desisting from gossip, rather than a sweet-sounding bromide, is a radical break with conformity. Rejecting gossip can do more than any other single step to make you feel at home with yourself. The anti-gossiper sometimes fears that he or she will grow boring or isolated. But if you try it, you'll see that neither conse-quence will befall you—indeed, you'll be more attractive to the right kinds of people. It is a nerve-inducing step.

Personally, I like works of spiritual self-help, such as *Alcoholics Anonymous*, because they encourage self-change on an epic scale. As discussed, I am less enamored of books that effectively instruct lowering your personal standards as a means to getting ahead, including being sneaky, claiming undeserved credit, and keeping colleagues and workmates off-balance or uninformed. As I've written elsewhere, a not inconsiderable number of headline-making studies in cognitive psychology rely on some of the same short cuts or oversold conclusions that researchers routinely accuse New Age writers of. This trend has weakened the current crop of psychological self-help books. But as far as the classics are concerned— by which I mean works that have attained posterity such as *How to Win Friends and Influence People* and *Think and Grow Rich*—their practical effectiveness rests chiefly on the passion of the individual seeker. That has been my experience in years spent circulating among self-help enthusiasts. And being one myself.

An Arab proverb goes: "The way bread tastes depends on how hungry you are." The depth of your hunger for self-change is likely to match the benefit you experience from any legitimate self-help program. This is because the individual's passion for betterment is a force of deliverance. That is perhaps the most actionable principle of human nature. Use it.

Action Step
My Favorite Prayers

I believe that prayer can be lifesaving. You may be able to identify a turning point in your personal experience where prayer rescued you from a crisis or clarified a serious problem. I believe in praying in whatever way speaks to your heart and psyche, and to whatever your personal conception of a greater power. I offer no instructions other than sincerity.

That said, I want to share with you two of my personal favorite prayers. These may be the kind of statements for which you've been searching, or they may supplement your existing practice.

I have long admired this prayer from Napoleon Hill, which you may want to recite daily. If it speaks to you, write it down on a card and keep it at hand:

I ask not for more blessings, but more wisdom
with which to make better use of the blessings
I now possess. And give me, please, more
understanding that I may occupy more space in
the hearts of my fellow men by rendering more
service tomorrow than I have rendered today.

You can address the prayer to a greater power, to Infinite Intelligence (as Hill often did), or use it simply as a meditation that speaks to your highest ideals.

Here is a radically ecumenical prayer from director David Lynch, which I also find deeply meaningful. He sometimes recites this statement at the end of his public talks. I had the privilege of asking David to speak it live during a public-radio interview. May its words enter and occupy your life:

May everyone be happy.
May everyone be free from disease.
May auspiciousness be seen everywhere.
May suffering belong to no one.
Peace.

Appendix A

Napoleon Hill's Seventeen Laws of Success

There are seventeen laws of success: these traits appear in the life of almost any exceptional person. Each Napoleon Hill Success Course explores one or more of these laws in detail. Although it is important to master all seventeen principles, the qualities of the whole are, in a sense, inherent within each one, the same way a primeval forest may be traced back to a single acorn.

1. **DEFINITE PURPOSE.** The starting point of all achievement is one definite, passionate, and specific aim. This is no ordinary desire, but something you're prepared to dedicate your life to. Your aim must be written down, read daily, acted upon constantly, and held in your heart with iron commitment.

2. **MASTER MIND.** This is a harmonious alliance ranging from as few as two to as many as seven people who meet at regular intervals to exchange ideas, advice, and sometimes meditations and prayers for one another's fulfillment. The Master Mind is critical to your success, as the pooling of intellects results in heightened insight, acumen, and intuition for all members.

3. **APPLIED FAITH.** Faith is learnable. If you take the nine concrete steps outlined in chapter eighteen you will discover that faith in your abilities and in unseen sources of help will bolster and fuel your effectiveness and persistence. Faith is the gelling factor that aids all of your efforts.

4. **GOING THE EXTRA MILE.** You are most efficient, and will more quickly and easily succeed, when you dedicate yourself to work that you love and that you find indistinguishable from leisure or play. When you work with this kind of passion, the quality and quantity of your work improve and you naturally do *more* and *better* work than you are paid for. This is why you owe it to yourself to find the work that you most like—and express that work by always going the extra mile for clients, customers, and employers.

5. **POSITIVE MENTAL ATTITUDE (PMA).** This does not mean blocking out bad news or cultivating an unrealistically rosy mindset. Rather, it means believing in your reserves of resilience, using

every positive tool at hand to approach your goals, and knowing that you possess or can acquire the necessary resources to deal with nearly any challenge. People with PMA naturally attract others and become leaders.

6. INITIATIVE. Leadership is essential to success— and *initiative* is the core of leadership. Initiative means *doing what ought to be done without being told to.* Only those who practice initiative become self-starters, examples to others, and high achievers. Initiative is one of Hill's simplest (if not easiest) laws; its practice is transformative.

7. ENTHUSIASM. Without enthusiasm nothing is possible. With it, you demonstrate acts of tireless commitment, which sometimes seem extraordinary. This is why your Definite Chief Aim must tap your passions. Enthusiasm is the closest thing life grants us to a magic elixir.

8. PLEASING PERSONALITY. Your personality is the sum total of your characteristics and appearance: the clothes you wear, your facial expressions, the vitality of your body, your handshake, your tone of voice, your diplomacy, your thoughts, and *the character you have developed by those thoughts.*

9. ACCURATE THINKING. Accurate thought is vital to success. Thinking accurately means relying on facts, observations, experience, and data that are relevant to your aim. This means shunning gossip,

rumor, hearsay, idle talk, and—above all—casual opinions from people who know little or nothing about your field.

10.   **PROFITING BY FAILURE.** What we call failure is often temporary defeat. Temporary defeat frequently proves a blessing because it jolts us and redirects our energies along more desirable paths. Reversals, setbacks, and temporary defeat impel the success-driven person toward improved actions and plans. Never miss an opportunity to review a disappointment for practical lessons and fresh approaches.

11.   **BUDGETING OF TIME AND MONEY.** A friend once observed, "If you don't know how much money you have you probably know very little else." You must keep track of and budget your two most precious outer resources: time and money. This means making a regular schedule of saving and paying down debts. It also means bringing orderliness to your tasks, knowing when to let go of a time-wasting activity, and honoring deadlines. Time is the one resource that no one can replenish or replace.

12.   **SELF-DISCIPLINE.** Self-discipline or self-control is the force through which your enthusiasm is directed toward constructive ends. Without self-control—in speech, action, and thought—your enthusiasm is like unharnessed lightning: it may

strike anywhere. The successful person combines both *enthusiasm* and *self-discipline*

13. **CONTROLLED ATTENTION**. This law relates to the two previous ones. You simply cannot afford the luxuries of a wandering mind (not always easy in the digital age) or procrastination. The latter is usually a form of fear, and it can be addressed through several of the methods explored in this book, including autosuggestion and possession of a Definite Chief Aim. "A man is what he thinks about all day long," wrote Emerson.

14. **TEAMWORK**. Success cannot be attained singlehandedly. It requires teamwork and cooperative effort. If your work is based upon cooperation rather than competition, you will go places faster and enjoy an additional reward in reduced stress and anxieties. To win the cooperation of others you must also offer them a strong motive or reward.

15. **SOUND HEALTH**. If you maintain indulgent habits of food, alcohol, or other intoxicants, these things will ultimately take over your time, your health, and your life. Your work and aims will eventually wither if you do not maintain reasonable habits of eating, rest, and exercise. If you do not pay adequate attention to your health now the consequences will claim all of your attention later.

16. **CREATIVE VISION.** Creative vision and imagination are the visualizing faculties that formulate your plans and *connect knowledge with new ideas.* Imagination and vision are not the equivalent of daydreams or escapism. Your imagination must be primed with credible information and facts, which it will then shape into ideas and applications.

17. **COSMIC HABIT FORCE.** This is one of Hill's most exciting and transformative principles. If you can train your habits of thought, emotion, and body along the lines of all the laws outlined above, an additional force—call it Infinite Mind, the Over-Soul, or Cosmic Habit Force—will lend itself to your efforts and provide an added boost to everything you do. Cosmic Habit Force expands who you are. It is the energy through which life replicates itself through established channels. Create the positive channels through which you want to express your life and Cosmic Habit Force will aid your advancement.

Appendix B

The Secret of
*Think and Grow Rich**

by Mitch Horowitz

Author Napoleon Hill refers to a "secret" that runs throughout his 1937 self-help book *Think and Grow Rich*. This secret, he writes, appears at least once in every chapter. But he does not specifically name the secret.

Hill writes that it is more beneficial and penetrating for you to arrive at the secret yourself. Some readers, he says, grasp it almost immediately. For others it takes multiple readings. Sometimes, right in the midst of a chapter, the secret may flash into your mind. It often comes, Hill writes, when you are ready for it.

I had such an experience recently. I found what I believe is the secret. In actuality, what I discovered is an expansion of something that I've written about

---

* Originally published at Medium on February 29, 2020.

earlier—but with a difference. I have previously written that the secret of *Think and Grow Rich* can be put this way: "Emotionalized thought directed toward one passionately held aim—aided by organized planning and the Master Mind—is the root of all accomplishment." I stand by that. But a more basic conception of Hill's secret reached me as I was revisiting Hill's section on "applied faith." It is this:

The "secret" of *Think and Grow Rich* is to place yourself within the overall scheme of creation, obeying natural laws that inevitably and invariably beget growth, expansion, renewal, and generativity.

Each step in Hill's work is designed to bring you into *natural, reproductive alignment with laws that enable nature and all of life.* This is not dissimilar to concepts found within Taoism and Transcendentalism. Once you are in alignment and work within this cosmic flow—toward continual growth and expansion—cycles of generativeness appear at your back.

You become like the seedling that eventually bursts through the soil. All of nature operates to make this growth occur. Unlike the seedling, however, a sentient being must consciously and selectively labor. That is your role in creation. But when you are productively united—mentally, emotionally, and physically—in the direction of your aim, you naturally enlist these reproductive laws. These laws possess greater potential for a conscious being than they do for the seedling *because they not only aid your expansion but also allow for a dramatic re-creation of self.*

I want to share what I consider the most important passage in *Think and Grow Rich*. It appears in the chapter on "Imagination" and directly pertains to what I've been referencing:

You are now engaged in the task of trying to profit by Nature's method. You are (sincerely and earnestly, we hope), trying to adapt yourself to Nature's laws, by endeavoring to convert DESIRE into its physical or monetary equivalent. YOU CAN DO IT! IT HAS BEEN DONE BEFORE!

You can build a fortune through the aid of laws which are immutable. But, first, you must become familiar with these laws, and learn to USE them. Through repetition, and by approaching the description of these principles from every conceivable angle, the author hopes to reveal to you the secret through which every great fortune has been accumulated. Strange and paradoxical as it may seem, the "secret" is NOT A SECRET. Nature, herself, advertises it in the earth on which we live, the stars, the planets suspended within our view, in the elements above and around us, in every blade of grass, and every form of life within our vision.

Nature advertises this "secret" in the terms of biology, in the conversion of a tiny cell, so small that it may be lost on the point of a pin, into the HUMAN BEING now reading this line. The conversion of desire into its physical equivalent is, certainly, no more miraculous!

In short, Hill maintains that you derive confidence, faith, a renewed sense of self, and authentic help from placing yourself within the cyclical scheme of creation, which is what the other steps in his book are designed to do. (I make my own prescriptions in my book *The Miracle Habits*.) This is the "secret" to which Hill refers. I would not recommend it unless I discovered its truth for myself. But you won't believe me until you try it. Which, in a sense, means his secret remains concealed.

Appendix C

Why I Am a
Think and Grow Rich Fanatic*

by Mitch Horowitz

I often use this blog to explore contentious issues in New Thought. But not today. Today I am writing as a fanboy—and with unashamed admiration for Napoleon Hill's *Think and Grow Rich*. I am a fanatic for the book. I give away copies, evangelize for it, and recently published a replica of the original 1937 edition.

Having beat a drum for *Think and Grow Rich* for years, I am sometimes asked by friends and coworkers: Does this brashly titled, 80-year-old self-help book *really* work?

The answer is yes. But only if you avoid one common mistake: reading the book casually, thinking that

_____

• Originally published at www.harvbishop.com on August 30, 2016.

you already "get it"—and thus skipping vital exercises and steps.

Think and Grow Rich will yield its magic only if you do exactly what the author says—and do it as if your life depends on it.

Maybe you're like me. You've read dozens upon dozens of self-help books and you have a "been there, done that" attitude. It is easy to fall into. But that kind of approach will blunt the benefits of *Think and Grow Rich*. This is because Napoleon Hill wrote the book in a very exact manner. He spent twenty years studying the lives of high achievers of all types—inventors, generals, diplomats, artists, industrialists—and he codified their common traits into a step-by-step program. Hill was certain, as am I, that he had created a model of what great minds do when bringing an idea from the conceptual stage to the physical stage.

When friends tell me that they feel stuck in life, I give them a copy of *Think and Grow Rich* with this advice: Go home and start reading the book, and follow every step and exercise with fanatical zeal. Forget about every other self-help book that you have ever read (including those that crib from *Think and Grow Rich*). As a personal experiment, dedicate yourself to Hill's process for six months.

One of the beautiful things about *Think and Grow Rich* is that it can be used to attain any worthy aim. Whether you're an artist, graduate student, or soldier, if you're not reading *Think and Grow Rich*, you're selling yourself short. The book will meet you wherever you are, and will serve whatever goal you have in mind. But only if you follow its program all the way.

Let me offer a personal example. Hill instructs you to write down a specific sum of money that you want to earn, and the date by when you want to earn it. When I first started reading *Think and Grow Rich* I was uncomfortable writing down a particular amount. I hesitated doing so. It felt unnatural. It seemed to me like I was closing off options or cheapening my priorities. Writing down a sum chaffed against my religious leanings. But once I got past those hesitancies, I found it extremely potent to commit to an exact dollar amount and deadline.

As I write these words I am looking at a yellow sticky note pasted inside the back cover of my personal copy of *Think and Grow Rich* (whose jacket and spine I have covered with clear packing tape to keep the book from falling apart after repeat readings). My yellow note is dated "11/23/14" and has a specific sum which I committed to earning by "11/23/15" (which happens to be my birthday). I later wrote an addendum on this piece of paper: "This happened!! 5/27/16." The latter date is when I noticed, quite by surprise, that the sum had arrived within the specified time frame.

Why did this happen? One reason is that writing down and committing to a precise amount and deadline can produce a unique pull on the mind, both consciously and, I suspect, subconsciously. When you write down, and thus reinforce, any concrete goal, you start noticing opportunities, people, possibilities, and ideas that can serve your objective.

So, accept my advice as that of a friend who wishes you success: Read *Think and Grow Rich* in the right way. Set aside all doubts and self-help fatigue, even if you've read it before. Give the book everything you've got. It will give back to you.

About Napoleon Hill

NAPOLEON HILL was born in 1883 in Wise County, Virginia. He worked as a secretary, a reporter for a local newspaper, the manager of a coalmine and a lumberyard, and attended law school, before taking a job as a journalist for *Bob Taylor's Magazine*, an inspirational and general-interest journal. In 1908, Hill interviewed steel magnate Andrew Carnegie who told him that success could be distilled into a set of practical principles. The industrialist urged Hill to interview high achievers in every field to discover these principles. Hill dedicated himself to this study for more than twenty years, and distilled what he found into his books *The Law of Success* (1928), *Think and Grow Rich* (1937), and other classic works. Hill spent the rest of his life documenting and refining the principles of success. After a career as an author, publisher, lecturer, and business consultant, the motivational pioneer died in 1970 in South Carolina. Learn more about Napoleon Hill and the Napoleon Hill Foundation at www.NapHill.org.

About Mitch Horowitz

One of the today's most literate voices in self-help, MITCH HOROWITZ is a writer-in-residence at the New York Public Library, contributing lecturer at the Philosophical Research Society in Los Angeles, and the PEN Award-winning author of books including *Occult America; One Simple Idea: How Positive Thinking Reshaped Modern Life*; and *The Miracle Club: How Thoughts Become Reality*. Mitch has written on everything from the war on witches to the secret life of Ronald Reagan for *The New York Times, The Wall Street Journal, The Washington Post, Salon*, Time.com, and *Politico. The Washington Post* says Mitch "treats esoteric ideas and movements with an even-handed intellectual studiousness that is too often lost in today's raised-voice discussions." He narrates popular audio books including *Alcoholics Anonymous, The Jefferson Bible*, and G&D Media's series of Condensed Classics. Mitch has discussed alternative spirituality on CBS Sunday Morning, Dateline NBC, NPR's All Things Considered, CNN, and throughout the national media. The Chinese government has censored his work.

This book is also available in an Ascent Audio edition narrated by the author.

CPSIA information can be obtained
at www.ICGtesting.com
Printed in the USA
JSHW061424160922
30598JS00002B/2